M000163525

WE ARE NOT
SHADOWS

WE ARE NOT
SHADOWS

Edited by
Hannah Fields

FOLKWAYS PRESS, LLC

Texas, USA
www.folkwayspress.com

'1999' first published in *Assembly Instructions* in 2019
'The Rest is Poetry: Why We Come Out' first published
in *My Pink Road to Russia* in 2015
We Are Not Shadows first published in 2021

We Are Not Shadows © Folkways Press, 2021
Interior and cover illustrations © Eviory, 2019

Printed and bound in the United States by
Bookmobile

ISBN-13: 978-1-7362701-0-3

9 8 7 6 5 4 3 2 1

CONTENTS

CONTENTS

WE ARE NOT
SHADOWS

INTRODUCTION

I'm absolutely thrilled to bring you the first
publication from Folkways Press and to know
that you've chosen to read the words compiled
inside. When thinking of what kind of book
I wanted our first publication to be, I knew I
wanted it to be something that carried a power-
ful message. I began the process by writing
down themes I felt were both timely and im-
portant, which, as you might've guessed, filled
an entire page. However, when I really sat
down and considered what was in front of me,
my mind kept trailing back to a conversation
I had with a friend about anthologies. During
our chat, she made the point that, while many
anthologies take on important topics, most
writers are usually in their twenties or thirties,
especially women writers. While it's wonder-
ful that young writers are having their voices
heard, many women writers over 40 are often
overlooked. That being said, my friend went on

to explain that she enjoys what young writers have to say but would love to hear from women her age or older, too. As I thought this over, something clicked, and I knew what I wanted to achieve with this anthology: bring together women from all ages and backgrounds to speak up and speak out about their experiences.

Though this was a generally broad idea at the time, the theme "We Are Not Shadows" developed when I began thinking of my own experiences as a woman. There have been times when my voice has felt small; times I wish I'd advocated for and stood up for myself more; times I've felt uncomfortable in a workplace or in a situation I wasn't sure how to get out of; times I've thought, "If I were a man, this wouldn't have happened or this wouldn't be the case." It was in each of those instances that I felt like a shadow, like something forgotten or overlooked unless it was cast in just the right amount of light. The more I thought about this, the more inspired I became to reach out to other women who've shared these feelings. I wanted this book to be a platform where women could discuss struggle, adversity, and challenges they've faced in their everyday lives – and that's exactly what it became.

When submissions started coming in, I noticed that many women noted in their emails that this was their first submission to a publisher or it was their first time submitting such personal work for the opportunity to be published. I value the bravery of each of them. It can be so difficult to put yourself out into the world and allow someone else to read something so close to you. Choosing which poems, essays, and stories to include was tough, as I would've included every entry if I could have. Even so, each word sent my way carries great importance and I hope each writer continues to use their voice to share their stories. The world needs to hear what they have to say.

As publisher of *We Are Not Shadows*, I'm honored that the writers you'll meet on the following pages trusted me with their words. It's been such a wonderful process working with each one of them. I especially love that these 34 women are of all ages, backgrounds, and countries. There are writers in their twenties and writers in their sixties. There are writers from the United States, Scotland, Saudi Arabia, New Zealand, and beyond. There are college students and educators and mothers and every title you could imagine. Though they might all be different in some way, they are united by the power of their voices and desire to come together and inspire each and every reader to step from the shadows and speak their truth.

It is also with sincerest gratitude that I thank every person who made this anthology a possibility, especially during the trials we've all faced during 2020. Starting a publishing company during a pandemic wasn't my plan, but I'm thankful for all those who continued to champion this book, even before its publication. It is my hope that you find hope and inspiration within these pages and that you face toward the sun to feel its light upon your face. You are a shadow no more.

HANNAH FIELDS
Publisher/Founder
Folkways Press

PROSE

OLD SONGS

by Isla Mani

Chanda Muma door ke
I repeat these sounds, not as words but as I
hear them. This is a song that comes from my
mother's tongue, not my mother tongue.
Puye pakaayen boor ke
There's no need for interpretation of the above;
this song is the composition of love. My mother's
love, a love that outside of this song always
needed translation.

A love that God must have thought was too rich,
so was spoon-fed in small portions, inch by inch.
As you would do for a malnourished child, in case
the food is too potent and leaves the body defiled.

Is that why she hid it, that I might reject her?
Purge her love from my system as she had been
pushed away so many times before. She was the

forgotten child. Just one of twelve and a girl. Not even worth the back of her father's hand. Her mother, widowed too early. She was raised by confused siblings, children who did their best but parenting even they themselves did not understand. So they're best left as memories that now reside forever on her skin. Their best was to teach her that emotion should be held deep within.

So, I was the greatest and worst thing to come into her life. As I was a dreamy child.
The dreamy child makes laughter a contagious disease.
The dreamy child loses lunch boxes, books, uniforms, and keys
The dreamy child lies and hides because apologies do not appease
The dreamy child takes cardboard boxes and turns them into comets
The dreamy child is slow to finish her meal
Has food shoveled into her mouth until she vomits
The dreamy child makes playgrounds from thin air
The dreamy child is never dressed on time
The dreamy child knows it's not the belt, but the glaze of fury in her eyes that she should fear
The dreamy child makes up stories to transport her outside this universe

The dreamy child fears silence the most because the dread of exclusion feels worse

But I am no longer a dreamy child, a forgetful or fearful child. I am an adult, who can screen phone calls to avoid toxic conversations. I can travel across oceans and contain visits home to short vacations, where the harm is easier to repair.

But daughters are indebted to their mothers, so often I am drawn back by her despair. Because, she is the foundation I stand on, and also my noose. So goes that continuous merry-go-round of abuse. So I find solace in the purpose God promises my future holds and torment in the virtues that I am supposed to uphold.
Honor thy Mother
Forgive those that sin against us
So time and time again, she and I rebuild trust.

With time we can gain clarity from pain and I see her now; I see her and I can see how we are the same. The cracks in both our structures have been reinforced with steel to survive. I see her now, a newer version, milder, transformed by chemical manipulation that has not subdued her but helped her to laugh, to breathe, forgive, to rest, to finally be alive.

I hear her now; I hear her sing *Chanda Muma door ke.* And I feel the steel barriers inside her breach from the volume of her yearning. I hear her sing, *Puye pakaayen boor ke.* It is like a torrent of affection that she cascades over my niece, who is innocent of the grief I feel, who can return her with a devotion that I can't yet reach.

As I am an echo of her and previous generations. How can I suppress our ancestors' perpetual reverberations? I can't extract what has been engrained inside, forget about childhood dreams where nightmares reside. So instead we sing sweet songs about uncle moon. Pretend we are new people, rejuvenated and vacant. Singing an old tune.

Bio: *Isla Mani is a queer, New Zealand born poet and spoken word performer of Indian and Scottish heritage. Her work is influenced by her personal experiences as a migrant of mixed-race heritage and by her professional work on social concerns in health, equalities and the environment. As a descendant of the indentured working system in the Pacific, this poem is about her experience of attempting to heal the wounds of intergenerational trauma.*

HOUSE RULES

by Neelim Dundas

Derry, Northern Ireland, 1978

I am lying on a black leather two-seater in
Auntie's house, staring up at a picture on
the wall. It is of Krishna. He looks as if he
is two or three years old. He is on all fours
on an island the shape of a bathmat. Other
small islands fill the black background like
silvery clouds, but my eyes are drawn to the
child festooned in gold jewellery; two neck-
laces; bangles; amulets; earrings; even his
peacock hair accessory has a gold fastening.
Krishna's luminous blue-white face contrasts
with his bright red lips and rosy cheeks. My
thoughts flit back to the sweets Auntie has
promised me. She is outside, hanging out
washing, and I figure I better remind her I
am still in her house.

Outside, it is sunny. Brightly colored saris dance in the breeze next to Uncle's boring, flapping shirts. My great-aunt smiles down at me.

"Are you going to marry an Indian man or a white man when you grow up?"

"White," I murmur. I think about my salmon pink dolls with blond or brown hair and feel I have given the right answer. I am only nine, but I sense that my reply is important to her. Was there a right answer? Auntie's expression gives nothing away as she continues pegging out clothes.

Looking back, I realize that as I was the first mixed-race child in the family, she was curious. Her nephew was the second one in the family to marry someone who wasn't Indian.

"Will you live in Scotland or stay here in Ireland?" she continues.

"Dunno." I can remember thinking *why does she want to know? Adults ask strange questions*.

I return next door to my Granny Comar's house. It is half past five and she is making *roti*.

"What did you talk about?" she asks.

"She wanted to know if I would marry an Indian man or a white man," I repeat.

Granny talks to Grandad in Punjabi. I guess that it is about Auntie. I can tell from her tight jaw that she is angry.

"Take your shoes off. You know you don't wear them in the house."

I take them off. When I stay with my Granny Herd over in Scotland, she lets me wear shoes in the house. She has different rules, but Granny Comar's rules are more important because we live with her at the moment.

St. Andrews, Scotland, 1978

My brother Neil and I are staying with Mum's parents for two weeks during the summer holidays. They fuss over us. I don't have to help in the kitchen like in Granny Comar's house. Granny Herd even makes us "supper," which we don't normally get at home. At breakfast time, she doesn't scold us if we scoop out jam from the jar with butter-smeared knives. We don't have to use a clean spoon for this, like in Granny Comar's house.

Neil and I are taken to the beach twice but mostly we play out in the big garden. One Wednesday, it is Granny Herd's turn to host a coffee morning. Her friends tell stories in loud, funny voices and have exaggerated expressions like children's television presenters.

One lady says, "It must be lovely having the children to stay, Isobel."

"I'd rather have them for a week than a fortnight," Granny replies.

Her friends all laugh. Another lady offers to bring us her grandchildren's Legos and her daughters' old annuals for Neil and me. We nod vigorously and give our best smiles.

Later, I ask Granny why she only wants us for a week. She loops her arm around my shoulders.

"Oh, you are such a sensitive soul. It is a saying, Caroline."

My Scottish family call me by my first name: Caroline. They don't know that Granny Comar calls me by my middle name, Suman, and now everyone else does too. I don't mind. I answer to both.

One day, I am keeping Grandad Herd company in his greenhouse. I stare at my hands and tell him that they are just like Mum's.

Grandad says, "Yes, but yours are the color of tobacco."

I don't like the sound of that. Even I know that tobacco is a dirty drug, something that is bad for you.

In the last week of our holiday, he takes me to one side.

"I think it would be nice if we got your granny a box of chocolates to say thank you for looking after you both. Granny is really tired, and it would be nice to show your appreciation. What do you think?"

"Okay, Grandad," I say.

I have never heard about giving presents for meals before. Now I have learned that it is expected to take a gift to someone's house. When we go to the supermarket, I ask Grandad to get another box so I can take it to my Indian granny. He says to get shortbread, as that is typically Scottish. On our last night, Granny Herd makes Chicken Marengo. My dad finds it bland, but he is back in Granny Comar's house having Indian food every night. I will miss Scottish granny's mince and potatoes and her cherry cheesecake.

Before we leave for Derry, we go to see Mum in Dundee Royal Infirmary. Just as we walk into the ward, she is showing a nurse a plastic wallet full of pictures of Neil and me. Mum's face is flushed as she is enjoying hearing the nurse complimenting us. When she sees us, her face lights up. She has multiple sclerosis, and it takes her a long time to speak. When Neil was younger, I could understand his baby talk better than anyone else. I don't understand Mum's words any easier, though.

She winks at me; I take her hand and hold it. I look at my grandad to see if he will comment on the color difference of our hands, but he is gazing at Mum.

"How are you, Margaret?" he asks softly.

Mum is tired from trying to talk and nods firmly to show that she is alright. An attached blue-and-white-checked table secures her in her wheelchair. There is a blue, gummy rubber mat in the middle of the table with a tumbler on top.

"What's that funny mat for?" I ask.

"It stops your mum's glass from slipping," says Granny.

Mum's mouth makes an O shape. She tries to catch the straw in her mouth, but it keeps twirling round the glass, out of reach. Granny leans forward and holds the straw so Mum can catch it between her lips. She drinks noisily, sits back in her wheelchair, pleased with herself.

Neil lies on the bed and quietly watching Mum. She raises a shaky hand and blows him a kiss. He smiles at her and blows one back. He then looks at me for reassurance. I can tell he doesn't remember Mum as well as I do. He never saw her walking.

Derry, Northern Ireland, 1978

We are back in Granny Comar's house and I have given her the box of shortbread to say thanks for making us food. She laughs, puts it on the work surface, and goes back to cleaning the cooker.

"You don't have to buy me anything. We're family," she says emphatically.

Neil edges over to the shortbread and tries to open the cardboard flap.

"After *roti*," she says.

Granny Comar expects me to help in the kitchen. It is my job to butter the *roti*. She rolls identical-sized balls of dough between her palms then lines them all up on the work surface. Then, with a rolling pin, she rolls one into a perfect circle, flipping it onto the hot plate of the *aga*. Expertly, with her bare fingers, she turns the *roti* onto its uncooked side before black speckles appear. She knows exactly when to turn it. I worry that I will never be able to make half the things that she makes. She lifts the rolling pin again and carries on rolling another *roti*, also keeping an eye on the one cooking on the hot plate. It fills with air. Granny daps it with a clean dish towel. I go over to her side and sniff the dough. It smells of home. I guess that Granny has made thousands of *roti* in her life and will probably make thousands more. I start dancing.

Granny looks up. "One minute dancing, one minute crying."

I stop dancing and go back to buttering.

"How many do we have?" she asks.

I open the folds of the dish towel in the *roti* box then unwrap the tin foil and count the soft discs of bread. There are seven, so she makes one more.

The *roti* melts in my mouth when we are all seated at the table, eating with our hands. We never do that at Granny Herd's house. The summer before, when Granny and Grandad Herd came over from Scotland, Granny Comar invited them to her house for a meal. They ate their *roti* with a fork and knife. I thought it was funny. They looked so stiff and awkward, sitting in their shoes, while everyone else was in their socks or Scholl's sandals.

Back at school, I see my two best friends again. I am not even sure they know that I live with my grandparents. I don't tell them about my sick mother or mention that she is in hospital in Scotland getting special treatment—something to do with diving equipment. I tell them about staying in Granny Herd's house, going to the beach, and being at a coffee morning. One day, they defend me when a boy in class calls me blackie. Other boys laugh. I cry on my bed when I am back home and tell Dad when he comes to look for me.

"Those boys will ask you out one day," my dad says, trying to console me.

I screw up my face. He tries to change the subject and asks me what I had for lunch. I tell him we had semolina but that I couldn't understand why the canteen ladies never serve us *saemia* for pudding. After all, it is another milky pudding beginning with the letter *s*. I tell Dad that my friend, Jane, has never heard of it. I feel sorry for her, glad that my granny makes it at home. Dad then explains that it is an Indian pudding.

I have stopped going next door to Auntie's house. Dad says that she just gives me sweets so she can find out things. I think about it and realize that she does ask me a lot of questions. I feel sorry for her as she has no grandchildren, but I don't want to be a spy either, so I stay away.

Granny Comar lets Neil and me have glacier mints from her larder and has started making us sugar *roti*, which is fantastic! Granny is superstitious. She believes that something bad will happen to a person if she praises them, but I can tell that she is pleased with my buttering of the *rotis*. She says she never had a daughter so she wants me to learn many things so I will be helpful to others. I prefer to play. Poor Mummy is over in Scotland and she has no say.

Grandad Comar watches me set the table, asks me to run the water for a while so the water in the jug is nice and cold. He tells me I am the best girl in the house.

Bio: *Leela Soma was born in Madras, India and now lives in Glasgow, Scotland, UK. Her poems and short stories have been published in a number of anthologies and publications. She has published two novels and two collections of poetry. She has served on the Scottish Writer's Centre Committee and is now on East Dunbartonshire Arts & Culture Committee and The Sottish Pen Women Writers Committee. Some of her work reflects her dual heritage of India and Scotland. She was nominated for the Pushcart Prize 2020.*

MAGDALENA'S SOCIAL POSITION ESSAY

by algae

INSTRUCTIONS

You are to write a short essay (as long as needed) explaining the various ways in which you may hold privilege or face discrimination. Markers include—but are not limited to—class, education, gender, generational status, nationality, phenotype, race, religion, or sexuality. This essay can be informal and does not require citations from class readings. Type your social location essay below.

Magdalena Estrella Castillo
Sociology of Latinos
Rough Draft No. 2
September 17, 2017

Howdy y hola! My name is Magdalena Castillo and I grew up in a large Mexican American community, literally right next to Mexico. Many people that I have met here at Texas A&M have expected that it was easy to find my ethnic identity within a largely ~~brown~~ Latino community. And while I feel close to my culture, I'm not sure I feel close to the identity that comes with it. Being Mexican American or Chicana or Latine has been a label I've adopted, but I'm not sure which is supposed to be the right fit.[1] Maybe I'm just not used to any of them. In this essay I will be exploring my identity through various markers in my life to see if I can find the label I best identify with. ~~Maybe this essay will make me feel less alone.~~

---

[1] These terms are completely arbitrary to me. I'm not entirely sure what the difference is between any of these. All I know is that I'm not supposed to call myself *Hispanic*—at least that's what my roommate told me. Something about that word having a history with colonialism, but if that's the case, shouldn't we not use most of the English language since it's all borrowed from other languages, right? That's imperialistic or something.

Class. Raised in a border town in Texas, I lived well off in a middle-class household. ~~Mi papi~~ My father made most of our family's income working as a teacher, while ~~mi mamá~~ my mom had a part-time job at one of the daycares in town and was the home's primary caretaker. Due to this economic advantage, I was always allowed to do things for fun; I joined clubs and sport teams even if I wasn't at all good at ~~soccer or baseball or basketball or tennis or golf or cheer camp or swimming or track or anything related to~~ athletic sports. In an area where the majority of people were ~~poor, no, underprivileged, no~~ of low economic status, there were also "perks" I felt at times awkward to take; free lunches and having required uniform five days a week were ~~annoying, I mean,~~ lackluster. But getting free dual- and concurrent-enrollment to community college and our local university over the summer was pretty cool. ~~Some of my classmates, even though they had the grades to take those free classes, couldn't afford the online homework access codes and instead worked long hours at the pipelines. My grades honestly weren't the best and I'm really happy they only transferred as pass/fail.~~ Now that I'm attending school full time, I receive academic scholarships mostly ~~so I really can't mess up anymore~~, but my parents still help with some expenses ~~even if it means taking out loans~~.

Education. While I am not a first-generation college student ~~since my father got his master's degree at the University of Texas Pan American a school that no longer exists and my mother's Mexican degree didn't transfer with green card~~, it has been difficult adjusting to Texas A&M because it is a predominately white institution with little to no cultural, ethnic, and racial representation in ~~top~~ elite positions. My high school had ~~only~~ a majority brown population, ~~and all of the stuff we learned in our classes was dumbed down, so when I got to college, especially a good college, I had to learn how to learn again. And I actually tried in high school!~~ and was divided into two large factions: the people who cared and those who acted like they didn't. The ones who openly cared were known as the try-hards; they had parents who worked for the school district, and were mostly active in marching band, track, or swimming. I would ask my dad for help, him having done the whole college thing already, maybe pick up a few studying tips, but he also went to school in the '80's when dorm rooms still had land-lines. ~~How do I ask for help with homework if he doesn't like the fact I got accepted to A&M with my major undecided?~~ Sadly, there has been so much technological advancement since then along with the fact that he studied a different discipline that asking for help is not necessarily feasible.

Generational status. I am a second-generation Mexican American on my mother's side since she was born in Mexico and third-generation on my father's side since he was born here, but his parents were born in Mexico. Growing up, labeling myself by nationality or ethnicity had always been a puzzle I was unable to solve; my mother forbade me to say I was a *mexicana* as I was not born in Mexico, ~~pero~~ but I was also told by my grandparents to not say that I was a Mexican American as I did not migrate from Mexico to America. ~~¿Qué más puedo ser? Everyone wants to label me one thing or another because of my skin tone. What else am I supposed to categorize myself as?~~ So recently Chicana is a term I've read a lot in this class, and while I don't know much about it, I feel like it is the one I want to be seen as.[2] Because of my generation, I grew up in a bilingual home, learning Spanish to communicate with my parents and English as a means to learn from the American education system and communicate with society. I like to believe I have a good work ethic modeled by grandparents, who worked long, hard hours in fields picking crops and have a sound foundation, economically as well as academically. This is contributed by my generational status, and the fact that I feel the expectations of my family members and their struggles to uplift them, which then fuels my anxiety and therapy talks that I'm not supposed to talk about in front of my grandparents because my mom doesn't want me to be judged by them.[3]

Geographical location. The struggles of

---

2 Chicana to me means being Mexican American while being disconnected to your "national" identity. Because I'm from the border I feel like I don't know what it means to really be "Mexican," but since I know what that culture is like, maybe not the history though I do want to learn it, I still want to be associated with that.

3 Chicano culture doesn't truly believe in mental illnesses, unless it's physical — like brain cancer; everything else, you're just making it up. I'm not sure if it stems from *machismo* or something, but anything that isn't external pain can't be justified to the only community. And in my experience, women are the ones who are more "susceptible" to this type of illness.

living in such a controversial geographic area also arose my senior year of high school, the year Donald Trump won the 2016 Presidential Election. This was a time where all of my neighbors, classmates, the people I grew up with became insecure about not only their own well-being, but of the people they knew, and they grew up with. There were people all throughout my country who believed that my ethnic group was the cause of their problems; Latinos were grouped together to mean "Mexicans," seen through a xenophobic lens as the "other," and marked as a scapegoat for social tensions; my ethnicity became a title I could no longer escape. Over the years my father's jokes about having to pronounce my last name in a *gringo* accent in college grew more serious.[4] ~~There was no need to be associated with Kate del Castillo, famous Mexican actress known for playing a narco on Telemundo's La Reina del Sur. And even though Amado Carrillo didn't have the same last name as me, my father was still terrified of any misconception.~~ Home was no longer a

---

4 My father wouldn't understand how much harder acting like I wasn't in touch with my culture would be to make friends when everyone else embraced themselves fully for who they were.

place of rich culture, it was a place where "il-legals" were detained, it was a place to establish political dominance over Mexico.

Sexuality. Additionally, as a lesbian my sexuality influences others' perceptions of myself, within a Mexican society and society as a whole that views heterosexuality as the norm and correct way of attraction, being a lesbian isn't something that I proudly state. ~~I'm not proud to be scared about people's possible reactions to my sexuality.~~ Growing up, I struggled with my sexuality given the ~~fucking~~ toxic heteronormativity of Chicano culture and my family's rigid religious views.[5] It was something I was never comfortable with; the media turned my Latina identity into a sexual icon—but something only men

---

5 Catholicism was the only way of life growing up. Every night my sister and I would kneel by our shared bed and pray to the crucifix hanging above us: *Ángel de mi guarda, dulce compañía, no me desampares, ni de noche ni de día. No me dejes solo que me perdería.* Even when driving in town we would pray before leaving the house and there was no, "*Pórtate mal, pero cuídate bien.*" Sunday school was not optional or a gateway for the grand *quinceañera* and even after receiving our first communion and confirmation, we still went and volunteered for the younger classes. There was believing in *La Morenita* and the Risen. Pope was basically a godfather even when my god-father was distant. Being a lesbian would kill them.

were to enjoy. And this icon was something I was not comfortable in playing into nor the fantasy of turning straight if I found the right *guy*. It wasn't until recent years that I was able to surround myself with my girl-friend and a small group of friends that were accepting of my sexuality; within this community I was able to express myself without fear of judgment and embrace my identity as a queer Chicana.

Identity labels. While I don't always feel comfortable within them, I find comfort in them. Within my mind, terms are constrictive, and because I will never fully experience colorism, classism, sexism, or racism in the same ways that other Latina women have or will face, I feel as though I will never be worthy enough of being *x* term. My social location, as a lesbian, Mexican American women of a middle-class and moderately well-educated household has given me access to opportunities that individuals from different socioeconomic backgrounds might not have. I would not be the Maggie I am today had I not had all these small consistencies in my life. Had my household income been slightly higher or slightly lower, I might've not had the same access to certain academic aspirations in my life; maybe I would've had more financial aid. Maybe had I been straight I would've fallen in love in high school and not gone to a school six hours away from home. If I were born in Mexico and not the US. I could have had a slight accent that deters from me gaining a stable job. The possibilities are endless. As meta as it may sound, all these small choices make me unique. All these interlocking events made me, me.

Bio: *algae is a recent graduate from Texas A&M University and has finished writing her creative thesis about Mexican-American experiences in the Rio Grande Valley. The submitted piece is an excerpt of this ongoing anthology and has specific geographic connections to her hometown: Roma, Texas. algae's flash piece "Witch of the Water Tower" was recently published in Fudoki Magazine's online platform.*

THE DAY MY BODY LEFT

by Lyndsey Croal

I woke up today in a different body.

The lights above me were bright—so bright that my head felt like fireworks had been ignited inside it, but not bright enough to shed any sense of familiarity on my surroundings.

The air was dry and sour, and there was a metallic taste in my mouth; the sort of taste you get when you haven't slept properly for three days and you've drunk too much coffee to make up for it.

As I lay there trying to make sense of it all, I padded my hands along the smooth and soft sheets. I was in bed. Not my bed, though. Just as I had somehow transported into someone else's form, I was now in someone else's room in someone else's existence.

I turned my head to get a better look to the side. A feather lay on the creased pillow next to me, barbs bristling out like veins, curled as if to protect its fragile body. Mum would say it meant a visit from someone who'd left us, or a part of an angel left behind as their body detached from the world. I reached out for it and pulled it delicately into shaking hands where it bobbed back and forth, vulnerable.

My knuckles were pale and there was a vague discoloration on my forearm, light purple like a birthmark. I brushed my thumb over it. The body I remembered didn't have a mark like this.

I sat up and let the feather fall in front of me. It floated slowly before eventually settling on the crevice of the sheet just above my knee. I looked around the room. Everything, like the feather, was pale and light—minimalist, a designer might call it; peaceful, even. White walls, white sheets, white frames, and a floor of oak, sanded and lacquered—smooth and flawless.

I lifted the sheet that was covering me. It drifted off, revealing two sticks of flesh that felt disconnected from me but that bent at the joints as I moved. The skin, like my arm, had dapples of purple. Maybe whoever's body I was invading was clumsy. Maybe they often walked into tables or chairs or those corners of the bed frame that always came out of nowhere and hurt the worst.

It took me longer than it should have to notice the other nameless body in the room. It shifted position, lying spread-eagled on the corner sofa by the window. It—*he*—lay with a sheet half-wrapped around him, bare and muscled calves sticking out attached to white socks. He grunted and moved his head so I could see the mess of hair, the stubble, a dash of red on his lips. A face I didn't recognize.

Wrapping a sheet around my alien form, I sat up, letting my legs hang over the bed, my toes stretching out as I tried to remember where my own legs had walked last.

I'd been out with friends, I think. A birthday party, free wine, a friendly bartender, and then … I woke up here, in someone else's body. The in-between was blank.

None of it made any sense.

Could I have hit my head somehow? Or was I dreaming? My head swam as I stood up and walked over to the window. As I pulled the silk curtains open, light and noise spilled out in an assaulting cacophony. I closed them again, leaving only a sliver of light. The body in the corner grunted but didn't wake.

Who was he?

Something about that dimple in the chin, the crooked nose … it was familiar, yet still. I took my time to tiptoe around the room looking for clues. There was a bag on the kitchen island, contents spilling out: lipstick, a credit card, mints, some coins, and a phone—I checked, battery dead. I laid the items out like they were pieces to a puzzle I didn't have the template for.

There was a charger by the kettle, so I plugged in the phone. After a minute of "spinning loading sign" it chimed on. On the front was a picture of someone I didn't recognize next to someone I did: my sister. But who was the imposter standing next to her? An arm round a shoulder, matching sunglasses, dark curls, and a wrist tattoo. *Just like* ... I looked at my own arm and found the dandelion tattoo. I rubbed my hand over it, confused.

As I stared back at the screen, notifications chimed in. One after the other after the other. From Mara—my sister: "Where did you go?"

Then, "Hey, can you answer your phone please."

"Seriously, this isn't funny, why aren't you home?"

"I'm worried. Call me."

Six missed calls.

My hand hovered over the endless notifications. I was about to try unlocking it so I could phone her and ask if she knew where my body had gone, but then there was a yawn and a sigh from behind.

I bundled the sheet over my form, spun around, and froze.

Nameless body sat up and looked at me with a crescent smile. "Morning, beautiful." His voice was hoarse but musical. The kind of voice I might have found attractive in my real body.

I didn't reply.

He stretched out and slithered over to the window, pulling the curtains open and cracking the window. "Quite the night." His words felt distant, drowned out by the noises from outside.

"Where am I?"

He laughed. "My flat. Don't you remember?"

I shook my head.

"I guess we had quite a bit to drink."

"No. I'm not supposed to be here, this isn't …"
My body?

"Don't worry. We had fun. I promise."

His words triggered a wave of nausea and I swallowed bile. "I need to call my sister." I turned and tapped at the phone. How could I get it to redial?

He walked closer, eyebrows knitted into a frown. "You'll tell everyone you had a good night, right?"

"I should go."

He stretched his arms out. The sheet fell off around him, his chest bulky, strong, twice my feeble size. "Come on … shouldn't we exchange numbers or something?" He pointed to my phone.

"No."

"If that's what you want," he said, cocking his head.

"I want to go home."

"But you had fun, though?" It felt more like a question than a statement, but there was a hint of assurance in his voice. Cockiness. He stepped closer. His hair was greasy, his breath stale with a hint of alcohol. An image flashed into my head— his face, his body, his hands on mine. The nausea surged and I ran to the bathroom, locked the door behind, then retched and threw up in the sink.

Looking at the face in the mirror, I tried to figure out whose body was staring back at me: smudged mascara in panda-eyed beauty, hair looking as if it had been backcombed, a V-neck shirt with a button missing at the top. I felt down to the midriff where a skirt hung loose and limp over hips that ached and legs that tensed. I looked at the reflection again, but still didn't recognize the bedraggled form.

There was a knock on the door from nameless body.

"I'm going to have a quick shower," I shouted in as calm a voice as I could muster.

"Suit yourself," he replied, and his footsteps drifted away, followed shortly after by the hum of a kettle.

I left my clothes in a heap on the floor, crumpled and creased, and stepped inside the cubicle. The space filled with steam as water cascaded over me. I hugged my arms around myself, trying to feel something of this strange body, but there was just an empty void.

"You okay in there?" nameless body shouted through, his voice with a hint of irritation.

I ignored him and closed my eyes. Where might my body have gone? Had someone somewhere woken up in my body wondering how they'd ended up in the cramped bedroom with eclectic colored furniture and photos across the wall detailing a life they didn't understand? How could we have swapped in the first place? I surely hadn't made some Freaky-Friday-style wish with a stranger—my life was pretty good as it was.

Another knock, heavier this time. "Hey … look, I really need to go out soon."

Clenching my jaw, I turned the water off. I gathered my crumpled clothes and made myself into something that half resembled a human, washing the makeup away with toilet paper, using my fingers to loosen my curls.

Dressed and as clean as I could make my alien body, I stepped out.

Nameless body held out a glass of water, keeping his distance as if I were an animal to be tamed. I shook my head, even though my throat was dry and sore.

I walked past him and unplugged the phone. The "redial" button thankfully worked, and I retreated to the window to make the call. Outside I watched a woman walk along the cobbled street with a yellow Labrador, the kind we'd had when growing up. I wished I'd woken up in her body instead.

The dial tone rang six times before Mara's voice answered, frantic on the other side. "Casey, where are you? Are you okay?"

I looked over at nameless body watching me, sipping his tea at the kitchen counter. "I don't know, I'm … I'm just a bit lost."

Her voice caught. "What happened last night? God, why did I let you leave? I should have stayed with you, but you looked like you were having fun and …" Her voice trailed off. "Are you okay?"

"It's fine, I'm fine." I paused. She'd seen me leave. "Did you see where my body went? I'm trying to … I mean … did you see where *I* went?"

Mara sucked in a short breath. "Casey, what happened?"

"I don't know."

"Where are you?"

"In a flat. But I've lost my body." I sighed. "I can't find it and I want it back. I want to go home, Mara."

"Go outside. I'll come and get you. Keep your phone switched on. I'll use find-a-friend."

"Mara, my head hurts and my legs, they don't feel like …"

"Don't panic," her voice was strained. "Just leave now and find a place to wait. I'll be there as soon as I can."

I pocketed the phone and headed toward the flat door, ignoring his eyes on me.

"Hey!" he called to me.

I hesitated. "What?"

"Your shoes and your bag?" He held them out to me, uncaring, relaxed.

I took them but didn't say thank you before exiting into the corridor.

Outside, more than one person looked me up and down before moving away, as if I was holding a bomb in my bag, not half a red lipstick and a pack of mints. I popped one of the mints in my mouth and found a bench halfway down a random side street, pulling my knees to my chest. A few passersby, including the yellow lab owner, stared, but none spoke to me or asked me if they could help me find my body.

When Mara arrived out of a taxi and saw me—imposter me—sitting on the rusted bench in the morning light, she burst into tears. I didn't understand why she should be upset when it was me who'd become detached from my body. The least she could do would be to help me find it.

She looked at me, held my hands in hers, and stroked my sodden hair back.

"I'm taking you home. Then we're calling the police."

Good, I thought as she led me away. Police could help find missing things. Maybe they'd know why my body left.

Bio: *Lyndsey is Scottish writer based in Edinburgh. She received a Scottish Book Trust New Writers Award for 2020 and is working on her debut science fiction novel. She enjoys writing speculative short fiction and has been published in a number of magazines and anthologies. Find her on Twitter as @writerlynds or via her website www.lyndseycroal.co.uk.*

TUNNEL VISION

by Leonie Charlton

I've only drunk half my tea but it's gone that lukewarm way which makes me almost gag—especially first thing in the morning—so mole-eyed I've moved onto Facebook. I need to get a handle on that; what am I doing checking Facebook before my eyes are fully open? I can't see anyway, a sign of aging, my vision blurry until I've had my coffee; the tea just toys with the possibility of bringing me round to the day. I switch off the bedside light—only for a few minutes; the snooze alarm will go off again soon. Sinking back down under the duvet, I feel a swell of total happiness; this is all I want, to be cocooned in darkness under the just-heavy-enough weight of feathers.

The phone scolds a vibration across the mattress to me. I've got to get up, move into the day with focus. I'm taking my daughter to the city for an appointment at the eye hospital, a two-hour drive away. We've made this journey countless times over the past fourteen years; since she was three, when her green almond-shaped eyes started getting red, before the world began to go blurry around the edges for her, and her gaze—straight and true—turned a little in on itself. I wish I could let her sleep now. She looked tired last night. I love to know she's sleeping; somewhere, deep down, I think I believe sleep is the miracle cure.

Dr. M arrives in a hurry, sweeps through the ophthalmology waiting room; his eyes pass over us, unseeing, then land on three women sitting together. He lifts them with his eyes and they rise, a single movement of sheer tights and slender bodies and expertly blended makeup. Now, in the small consulting room, these women are standing by silently, their bodies a black-skirted bracket around Dr. M. He scoops into his chair with a rush of air.

"Well she did alright in the eye test just now." There's an accusatory tone in his voice.

"She knows the letters off by heart. She's been coming since she was three and they've never been changed." My voice is strung tight, ready to snap.

"You have an appointment scheduled for Monday, I don't know why you're here. I haven't got time for this." He's looking nowhere in particular.

"Dr. M, we're here because you told your secretary to tell us to come down today to the emergency clinic." The insertion of his name cuts through the air.

I think about my daughter calling me yesterday morning: *Mum, I can't see anything. It's never been this bad before … I can't read. I can't write. I can't do anything.* I want to say to Dr. M that she never complains, never; that for her to make that call meant it was serious. Tears slip down my face. I want to say more to him, to ask him what he would do if she were *his* daughter. I stop myself.

I reach across to the box of tissues meant for patients. Frustration burns my heart like a lightning strike. Frustration at Dr. M's indifference, at my own loss of control; how can I cry when my daughter doesn't, my brave and beautiful daughter who puts up with deteriorating sight and a lifetime of drops: Predsol, Pred Forte, Opatanol? Who puts up with microscopes and tonometers and slit lamps that make her eyes pour with tears? Who smiles at the strangers who stare into her eyes and never see her? The occasional consultant has taken time, and real care, and I've wanted to tell them I love them for their humanity, that they are angels for being attentive. And then they're gone. And today, here with Dr. M, with his shiny shoes and glossy eyes, I ask myself what could be the cure for his tunnel vision? I would love to help him, but I've run right out of empathy.

Now he and my daughter have gone down the corridor to get new drops. I turn to the three women; I scan for eye contact. Nothing, or I miss it in the blur of my tears.

"She's never done this before you know … had an emergency appointment." My voice sounds damp and pathetic.

They make conciliatory sounds. Maybe they're embarrassed—these three ophthalmologists doing work experience—who one by one had examined her, and who one by one hadn't said a word. Maybe they are full of compassion—had seen her suffering laid bare across the scarred surfaces of her corneas—but, like me, feel silenced. I should ask them, while we are alone like this, if they have any idea of what could help her. But I am too busy arranging my face into a smile, struggling to be polite and thankful; fearful that I might have made *him* angry, I am already sliding back into old patterns of good manners at any cost.

"I'm sorry I got emotional in there." I say in the lift on our way out.

"Don't worry, Mum. I think you did well. I was crying too, but nobody noticed because of the drops making my eyes water."

Back in the car I know that something has changed. My heart is singed with rage. My feathers are more than ruffled. Next time, Dr. M, we will be prepared. We will have questions, written down clearly in case tears blur the page. And I will bring my own tissues, and I will keep my beady eye on you. Who knows, maybe I am your angel come to help you see what people say with their eyes, and maybe you are *my* angel, come to teach me to stand up for what matters.

Bio: *Leonie Charlton lives on the west coast of Scotland. She writes creative non-fiction, poetry and fiction. Her work has appeared in publications such as Causeway, Northwords Now, and The Blue Nib. Her first full-length book, Marram, was published by Sandstone Press in March 2020. Marram is the story of her journey through the Outer Hebrides with Highland ponies; the travelogue is intercut with intimate memoir as she leaves behind beads in memory of her mother. Leonie won the Cinnamon Press Poetry Pamphlet Prize in 2020 and her pamphlet "Ten Minutes of Weather Away" will be published in early 2021. Much of her writing is based on a sense of place and our relationship with other species and the natural world. Learn more at www.leoniecharlton.co.uk.*

SCOOCH.

by Chiara Bullen

She's walking with her head bowed low against the biting cold, sleet slashing her exposed brows. Bags for life crammed with dinner make her back ache. She can just see the figure in the distance, directly in front of her, walking into her path amongst the bustle of Byres Road.

A man.

I won't move this time. She's sick of always making way for men on paths, in queues, in clubs, in shops. Moving out of their way as they usurp her claim to something as simple as space.

The bags are digging into her hands and sticking out with bulk. Surely, she thinks, she'll be victorious here. Surely she's the one who has the right to keep walking.

She estimates five seconds before they meet.

He shows no signs of moving.

49

A bump to the shoulder. "Watch it!" he shouts as he turns, ruddy-faced and hands in pockets.

"Sorry."

* * *

She pulls the handles of her bags up to the inside of her elbows so she can clutch her ticket and phone. Her arms are tingly from the weight, cutting off circulation. When she sits down, she'll rub the feeling back into them.

The orange blur of the subway carriage pulls in, the breaks shrieking and screaming in that old and tired way. When she was wee, she was told a banshee lurked the tunnels, yowling as the train went by. Every time she's here, she vows to invest in those noise-canceling headphones. But have you seen the price of them?

She doesn't realize how busy the platform is. Bumping and pushing ensue, folk trying to get home four minutes before the next train gets here. She finds herself shimmying up the middle of the tiny carriage. Packed like sardines is a cliché, but in these carriages with the brown, reddish glow, she's hard pushed to think of any other way to put it.

She really wants to sit, but the two rows of dusty seats are rammed. She can feel the first beads of sweat slipping down her back, underneath her t-shirt, jumper, and jacket. Dropping the bags to her feet with an air of defeat, she reaches for the germ-infested handrail above. She braces herself for the jolting movement of the journey.

There's a whole line of people standing and a bunch huddled by the doors. Glistening remains of sleet rest on puffed-up parkas, the floor wet from stamped boots and scuffed trainers. An inky black drowns the windows as they enter the tunnel, forcing her to examine her distorted reflection.

Wanting to look at anything else, she looks down at the man in front of her.

He's taking up two seats.

She realizes it with such intense ferocity she has to grip the handrail tighter as the dizzying fury unsettles her balance. She averts her gaze a little, scared he'll feel the heat of her scrutiny.

He's wearing a black overcoat, unbuttoned to reveal a crisp white shirt below. Concealing most of his torso is the broadsheet he's reading, which he's opened to the fullest. Doing so in such a cramped space means the pages may as well have the wingspan of an albatross. She begrudgingly

appreciates his support of the print industry—
when was the last time *she* bought a paper?

But back to the matter at hand.

It's the "manspreading" that really gets
to her. Those legs, spread open luxuriously
wide as if lounging on a sofa, remote in hand,
steaming tea on an IKEA end table next to
him. A small briefcase rests between his feet
on the floor, smug and supported leaning
against the seat. Her garish blue bags full of
shopping lean against it, the milk carton bul-
ging out the top.

She thinks of the man on the street. How
"sorry" slipped out of her so naturally, like
breathing, as the instinct to remain small and
safe overpowered her desire (and right!) to keep
walking in her chosen direction.

It won't happen again.

The way she sees it, she has three options.

The first one isn't actually doable, but it's her
favorite.

She glowers down at the spreader, eyes
glowing red. A mist seeps in from the cracks
in the carriage doors and the other com-
muters move away, startled. The man looks
up at her. The sheer intensity of her gaze, her
presence in this space, causes him to cower

behind the pages of his newspaper. Every pregnant mother, every luggage-burdened passenger, every disabled person ever forced to stand because of manspreading suddenly fill the space of the commuters who fled. A crescendo of rage-induced energy sweeps through the space. Even the banshee lurking the tunnels quietens in the wake of it. The spreader, eyes glassy, whimpers, "Would you like this seat?"

The train screeches to a halt at Cowcaddens. She shakes her head. Yeah, no. Option one isn't strictly possible.

Bodies push against her once again as more wet, steaming commuters stream through the doors. Peering between the woman's frazzled hair next to her and a sea of hats, she notices a pregnant woman board. She looks back at the spreader. He hasn't even looked up to check if anyone needs a seat—the bastard.

A lurch throwing her sideways means they're on their way again. Subway rides in Glasgow are notoriously short. If she waits any longer, she'll miss her chance to teach this guy a much-needed lesson.

Option two would be doable if her crippling anxiety would let her do it.

It goes a little like this:

"Oi, you."

Spreader looks up. "What?"

"Gonnae fucking move? You're taking up two seats."

"Oh. Sorry."

Scooching ensues. She offers the seat to the people around her, selflessly, but they refuse. She won the space fair and square, asserting dominance and making this man feel small. The essence of triumph would ooze around her as she took his seat. Someone would mutter, awestruck, "She's got big dick energy!" as she settled in place.

Blinking back to the present, she observes the sheer size of the man. The constant scowl as his eyes roam the page. She imagines them crawling over her skin as she initiates the conflict that, although a little unnecessary, would be the only way to release her anger and sense of injustice. She imagines him shouting back. Getting off the carriage. Following her home. Or finding her on Twitter. Getting doxed. Losing her job. Being targeted by trolls.

Yeah, no. Option two isn't doable either.

So that leaves option three. Not the best option, not the worst. Even though it's amicable, he could still react badly. At least she couldn't be accused of being rude.

She takes a breath, feels the sweat gather under her armpits and down her back. Her inner arm aches from holding onto the handrail, but she can't quite let go. Not yet.

"Excuse me," she utters, the words almost lost to the banshee. The spreader turns the page, dramatically putting his hands together before fiddling for grip then pulling them apart. She clears her throat.

"Excuse me!"

He looks up, blinks. "Yes?"

The people next to her are watching now. The men on either side of the spreader are looking up too. With all these eyes, the heat she's experiencing increases tenfold. She'll be *stinking* by the time she's home.

"Would you mind moving over a bit, so I can take a seat?"

The adrenaline that rushes through her makes her glad she kept hold of the handrail.

"Oh! Sure."

The newspaper is folded up. He lifts his briefcase to his lap and edges closer to the man next to him. This sparks a domino effect, and the men next to him scooch up too.

Disbelief. She's done it! His arse is actually moving! She quickly glances to those around her, a silent *do you want this seat?* But everyone has lost interest now, and even the pregnant woman isn't looking up from her phone.

It's settled then.

She twirls on the spot and plonks down, smiling.

Bio: *Chiara Bullen is a 25-year-old writer based in Glasgow, but she is from one of those rural Scottish villages you'd expect to see on Outlander. She has an honors degree in English Literature and Linguistics from the University of Glasgow. Chiara won funding to pursue a Master's degree in Publishing Studies at the University of Stirling in 2016, and has recently been awarded funding to conduct her Ph.D. there. For the past three years, she's been working as a freelance writer and with independent publishers, arts charities, and authors.*

THE LIZARD

by Ethel Maqeda

I wake up to a commotion outside on the street.
I strain my ears and hold my breath. It is some-
thing I do very well. I usually listen for a few
seconds then jump up, shouting "fight" or "ac-
cident" or whatever I figure the noise to be. I'm
usually right. Uncle and Ma do it too, but they
don't jump up and bolt out of the door like they
have been stung by *shungushungu*. Uncle ambles
out a little while after me, a frown of feigned
irritation on his face, looking like he is going to
ask what the fuss is all about and tell everyone
to go home or to take their noise somewhere
else. But he doesn't.

To understand what the commotion is about
quickly, you need to approach the heart of the
racket the way Uncle does, deliberately, listening
to what people around are saying, and cautiously,
in case you need to run away at short notice,

but I hate missing the beginnings of things and then having to rely on other people to fill in the gaps. Other people always manage to make themselves part of the story. That's how people, adults, retell what happened. They'll say, "I was just washing my husband's uniform. He is a soldier, as you know ..." or, "I had just sat down to eat my lunch, I was early today. I'm usually still cooking at this time ..." Sometimes they get so lost in their own story that I don't get to know what happened because in their story they might see a love rival in the crowd of people watching the action you missed and start to tell you about all the things she has been saying about them and how they are going to have it out with her in front of everyone, one of these days. If you manage to steer them back toward what you want to know, then they just say, "Then I heard the Santana arrive and I went back to my washing. Can you believe it? Those naughty Shumba boys knocked my pail over and ran away laughing. I'll have to have a word with their father. He should teach his children some manners instead of letting them run loose in the township. Why doesn't he have a wife, anyway?" I would have to just stand there and listen because you can't walk away when your elders are still talking.

So, although I like gossip myself, I prefer to see events as they happen and listen to gossip when nothing else is happening.

Ma comes out of the house last, always. She does so when she is sure there are other women already there. She almost always has to rely on me to tell her what's happened, so all she gets is, "Some policemen came to arrest the Rastas at number 1429. The Rastas at number 1429 refused to get arrested, so people booed and chased the policemen away. Then a Santana came with more policemen, and that's when you came out." She gets the abridged version all the time because she doesn't want people to think that she is a gossipmonger, so she nods too vigorously and says "hooo, hooo, hooo" so loudly I tell her the story in one breath.

Commotions are not uncommon in the Township. Also, our house is a T-junction house, directly in front of where two roads—Liboho Road, and the gravel road with no name—come together. There is no sign saying our road is Liboho Road, but Father says the papers that came with the house said our address is 1431 Liboho Road. No one is sure where the plaque stood or whether there had ever been one, but the most accepted and retold story is that

Mapostori stole the sign for scrap metal a few days after it had been installed. Mapostori love scrap metal—perhaps something to do with living off the land like the Apostle John the Baptist, whose teachings they follow. So, although no one has seen the sign or my father's or anybody else's papers, our road is called Liboho and the gravel road has no name. I have even given our address to a pen pal in Czechoslovakia as 1431, Liboho Road, Mkoba Township, Gweru, Zimbabwe, Africa, The World.

My mother is always dusting the furniture while humming tunelessly. She had wanted a corner house. The dust from the gravel road clings to everything in the house and the patch of the street directly in front of our house is also the meeting place for people who live on the two streets. It is the arena for all the dramas that happen on the two roads and sometimes commotions from nearby streets find their resolution in front of our house as well. This is how I have become an expert on the sounds of the street. Also, you just have to learn at an early age, because if, for instance, your fourteen-year-old friends call for you to come out and play *pada* or *nhodo* and they sound too nice, like they're pleading then you know that if you do go out, you have to be prepared to fight and not to play *nhodo* or *pada*. It means that something has happened, and you have lost a friend somewhere between the last game the previous day and waking up in the morning. Otherwise their normal call to play is impatient and full of threats to come out quickly or the game will start without you. Reading the noises of the street is a matter of life and death, my brother, Chipiwa, says. "The hunter must identify with exactness the various sounds heard in the forest." In the fourteen years I've been alive and lived on this street I have almost become as good as my brother.

A single long, piercing whistle, from the back of the house, just after supper, seems to be his call to go out hunting. I have never seen the whistler of this long, piercing whistle, but I think whoever it is must have been a cattle herder at some point in his life. Chipiwa doesn't make it back until long after we have gone to sleep. A similar sounding whistle, during the day, is for my sister, Chiedza, to put Vaseline on her lips, a bit of black shoe polish on her eyebrows, and wear her best shoes before going out. I have often wondered if the cattle herder and Chiedza's whistler are the same person. She gets back in time to make supper, which she does smiling to herself. I don't care about hunting or the single whistlers. It's the thunderous cheering, booing, and chorus of whistling—definite indications of a fight, a brawl, or a scantily-dressed-woman-walking-down-the-street fight—I don't want to miss. Sometimes when it's women fighting, they might tear each other's clothes off, or something unusual might fall out of a bra. Occasionally when nothing else is happening, children will follow a mad person and cheer, boo, and whistle while the mad person makes faces, dances, or makes sudden, threatening movements. Sometimes it's when a husband has found his wife with another man and makes the man leave the house naked while beating him. The husband might allow other people to join in with the beating, especially if the naked man is fighting back. If it's a woman who has found her husband with another woman, then the other women don't wait to be asked to help. They just join in, to teach the mistress not to steal other women's husbands. A husband and wife fighting is a "domestic." There is laughing and cheering, but no one tries to stop them. Even the police come and park their Santana a distance away, get out, lounge against the bonnet, and pull their caps down low to stop themselves from cheering.

Raucous laughter, whistling, and even louder cheering means there is a police chase—one or two policemen chasing a pickpocket or a shoplifter with a huge crowd of mostly children and young men following at a distance shouting "*mbavha, mbavha!*" The laughter is because the police officers, usually fat and unfit, are out of breath and will not catch the thief. The cheering makes it more fun, like at a football match.

Singing and drumming mixed with shouting from one person is a religious revival, *mvuserero*. The various churches are all agreed that our township is the modern-day Sodom and Gomorrah so they often, at different times, on different days, parade through the streets singing, get to a corner and stop. One person will start to shout, imploring people to turn to the Lord and be saved, for the second coming is nigh.

The loud exchanges between two women quarreling over whose turn it is to sweep the yard or apply *cobra* on the veranda, dogs barking, children laughing, a street vendor shouting his wares, and someone playing Gregory Isaacs on a ghetto blaster means everything is okay, there is nothing unusual happening. You could go outside and lean on your gate or sit on the metal bin and wait for something exciting to happen.

Complete silence means you don't go outside, or you take extra care if you do. Usually, only Uncle goes out to investigate. He doesn't do it immediately. He will hesitate until Ma laughs her spiteful laugh and then he will straighten himself to his full height and walk out as if he was marching at a parade.

People in our township spend a lot of time outside, on the streets, on street corners but particularly in front of our house, it seems to Ma. They only gather indoors when someone is going to die. Then, they wait and talk amongst each other in hushed tones. Once the waiting is over, the women then go outside wailing and throwing themselves to the ground.

Every important discussion and information exchange happens on a street corner. The street corner adds much more credence to a piece of information than a courtroom, the news, or church. I know this because everyone knows that in court you just say you know nothing, and you haven't done the thing that they say you have done and swear on your dead mother's grave even though she's still alive. That is what Uncle says. He knows about the law. He had a big book about the law which his wife used to hold down the tablecloth on the outside table where she used to sell boiled eggs and oranges. She is dead, and Uncle lives with us now.

People don't trust what they hear in church either, although they flock to the different churches throughout the weekend: *Johanne Masowe yeChishanu* (John the Baptist Friday), *Johanne Masowe yeMugovera* (John the Baptist Saturday), and all the other mainstream Saturday and Sunday varieties, Catholic, Methodist, Salvation Army. Ma says you have to have someone to bury you with dignity when you die, and that church people know how to do that very well. So, everyone goes to church. I was in church once when a man, moved by the spirit to witness and bring his sins before the Lord and lay them bare, confessed to having done all sorts of horrible deeds before he found the Lord. "I was a fornicator," he had said to tut-tutting and shaking of heads. "I was a murderer" to more tut-tutting and head-shaking. "I was a robber." No one looked horrified or shocked. Instead, the congregation had burst into "Lord Jesus, take my heart and wash it until it is as white as the cold," singing jovially and stamping their feet. Everyone knows that church is not a place for telling or hearing the truth, so no one asked him who he had murdered or who he had fornicated with.

If he had, in the course of socializing at a street corner, told a friend or a neighbor all the horrid things he said he'd done, the response would have been different. There would have been whispers, people would have crossed the street to avoid meeting the murderer and fornicator, and an attempt would have been made to convince the police to investigate.

People don't believe the news either. They watch the evening news and immediately go out onto the street to compare their reading of the events presented. "It's ZBC, your one and only family favorite station!" One of them will say, "What do you expect?"

"BBC, CNN, ZBC, all the same. All of them liars," someone else will say.

At which point the first one will say, "The ZBC doesn't have to lie to us. We can see it with our own two eyes."

"At least ZBC lies are our lies and not Britain's lies."

This will go on for a long time, until someone else says, "Ecclesiastes one verse two, vanity of vanities, and all is vanity," in English, and then it will be time to go in. It is the same every evening.

Our house has most of the benefits of a corner house without being one. The only thing we don't have that most corner houses have is a bigger garden. We also forego the benefit of not having neighbors on one side. I still think our house is better than most corner houses in the township because a small bridge, a culvert actually, runs over a small, stagnant gully that cuts across the gravel road without a name. A concrete bridge, however small, with small concrete ledges on either side gives our T-junction a status almost equal to that of a crossroad. Men sit on the ledges and talk for hours. Sometimes someone's wife, mother, or sister brings out roast peanuts and *mahewu* for the men to drink. We can play on the street, but us girls are not allowed to stand at a street corner for long periods in the same way the boys can go to the shops but are not allowed to play *slaag*. We can, however, sit on the ledge during the day because Ma can see where we are from the window. We can sit there until the men start coming back from work and we have to go back inside.

Although the gully underneath the bridge floods in the rainy season, for most of the year it is dry, and my father burns our rubbish in there. There is a bit of water in the gully from the thunderstorm the previous week; it is just nearing the end of the rainy season. The commotion outside is because a monitor lizard has been spotted in the gully. The lizard must have been washed in during the thunderstorm. My father would say that.

Monitor lizards, like hyenas, are associated with witchcraft. Hyenas are said to be ridden by witches at night for transport from one witching job to another. I found out about this on a bus one afternoon. The bus had failed to stop at a rail crossing. A woman asked the driver, "*Ko nhai mukwasha, ko* you didn't stop at the rail crossing?"

"Did the hyena you were riding last night stop at the rail crossing?" No one said anything after that.

As for monitor lizards, no one I've asked can explain a clear association to witchcraft. Monitor lizards are rare anyway; in the city, almost unheard of. Some *born location*. People who had never been to the rurals had never seen one. The only bad thing I've heard is that they love to steal milk from livestock, depriving hungry families of precious milk from their goats or cows. I find this both revolting and terrifying. I imagine that the cow or goat must be horrified when they realize that a different species is suckling from their breasts.

On this early morning, when I bolt outside to see what the commotion is about, I do it too quickly and people square their shoulders and elbows so I can't quite see anything. The crowd is unusually bigger. The men with jobs have not left for work yet. Someone tells me it's a very big lizard. People are standing in clumps talking. A man, in khaki trousers and safari shirt, is at the center of the crowd, someone tells me. I can hear him.

"I was on my way to work. I've never been late in all my life. This is not a good sign. My enemies have sent this lizard so I can lose my job. Oh, my poor mother! How … how am I going to look after my poor mother?"

"Stick to the point, VaMakhaki," someone shouts, and he gets back to the story.

He had come out of the house and locked the door. As he turned to start walking down the road, he caught a glance of something moving in the water. At first, he'd thought it was a crocodile. The crowd bursts out laughing.

Uncle, who knows a lot of things because he passed his Standard Six and always wants to take charge of situations, has already gone back into the house and called the wildlife and forestry commission all because a few people were beginning to clamor for the killing of the lizard. He is a spoil sport.

"It's a criminal offense," he warns them, in English.

Another group of watchers are speaking in whispers, their heads together, a little way away from the main crowd. I can only hear the words ZESA, occasionally. ZESA is the electricity supply authority, but if you live in our section of the township, Zesa is the nickname given to an old woman who people suspect of being a witch. She had been run out of her rural home and resigned to continually starting over in different townships. Her family had been "Muzorewa's people," *madzakudzaku*, when Zimbabwe had been Zimbabwe-Rhodesia for a few months in 1979. That's what everyone says. Muzorewa had become prime minister for a few months after coming to some agreement with Ian Smith. Although Muzorewa had disappeared into obscurity soon after independence, those who had supported his politics of compromise were forever tarnished, with no hope for forgiveness. They were *madzakudzaku*, traitors to be despised unto death. They could not just disappear into obscurity into some low-density suburb like Muzorewa. She could have kept running, gone where nobody knew her and started afresh again, but she had grandchildren who needed her now. Their parents had long disappeared to places where no one knew or would ever know Muzorewa.

I don't think anyone knows for sure that the old woman had been a Muzorewa supporter, but she is ancient and rarely smiles. She has a long, haggard face, which makes me think of a crocodile or a monitor lizard every time I see her. It is not so much the folds of her wrinkly skin but her eyes, big, gray, and lifeless. I think that many people who dislike her do so because they don't understand why so many people die young in the township and she doesn't. They know about AIDS and alcohol, everyone does. They don't know what to do about AIDS and alcohol, but at least they can get rid of witches. That's what my history teacher has said. "History is full of women condemned for daring to outlive the men in their lives," she'd said.

I smile at the old woman whenever our paths cross, willing her to do the same. If she smiles, I think, people might forgive her the Muzorewa thing. I want her to smile and shout a cheery hello, and then people might forget. I think she is a harmless old woman who has no reason to be cheerful. I can't say this to anyone. They might think I'm a witch too.

By the time the man in the khaki suit finishes his story, the smaller, separate group have already decided what they are going to do.

Shouting, mixed with singing, is the noise I fear most. It is the sound of an actual hunt, a group of people, usually the youth wing of a political party, singing *Chimurenga* songs until they spot the enemy. They stop singing and shout at the person to stop or to come out of their house. There might then follow catcalls and cheering—and prolonged screaming. It means a *perm*—chasing, general harassment, humiliation, beatings, and burning of houses—is in progress.

Chimurenga songs are the songs that won the liberation war against the British, everyone knows this. I love *Chimurenga* songs, the rhythm and the *toyi toyi* dancing that goes with the singing. Everyone loves *Chimurenga* songs, but I only like to see them sung on TV on national days of commemoration, like on Independence Day. When the breakaway group starts singing *"mupanduki chera mwena, mupanduki nguva yakwana"* (traitor dig a hole, traitor, your time is up) I know a *perm* has started and rush back inside, wondering if the old woman will survive the *perm*.

Bio: *Ethel Maqeda has lived in Sheffield since 2005. She keeps a strong connection with her home country by writing stories inspired by Shona and Ndebele storytelling traditions. 'The Lizard' portrays an instance of the gendered nature of Zimbabwe's current struggle for democracy. Ethel's short stories have appeared in a number of issues of Route 57, the University of Sheffield's creative writing journal, Verse Matters, (Valley Press); Chains: Unheard Voices (Margo Press) and Wretched Strangers (Boiler House Press). When she's not writing, Ethel works in an FE college supporting students with additional learning needs and relaxes by going to the theatre.*

ESSAYS

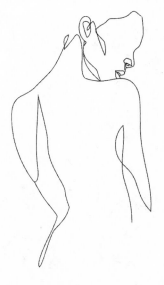

AIRFLOW
OVER OGIVAL WINGS:

AN AERODYNAMIC STUDY[1]

by Nicola Pitchford

My mother was never wild, but she was fearless.

As much as I loved her, as I longed to be with her, I also wanted her to be a *Wuthering Heights* mother; a river running free; a white witch. She was, almost always, sensible.

The first time I wrote about her, in full teenage earnestness, it was as a silver birch tree in a storm. I had in mind a particular slim birch in our old back garden, with beautiful papery bark that we children had to resist the temptation to peel. We were blessed with trees in that garden; the house had been built on a parcel of land that was previously part of a much larger es-

---

1 The title of a scientific paper cowritten by my mother and published by the [British] Aeronautical Research Council

tate, owned by a man who had created his own modest sort of arboretum. So we had an American dogwood in the middle of the lawn; a vast flowering magnolia at the bottom corner of the steeply banked garden, under whose low-hanging branches we made forts and hidey-holes on the dry earth; a row of prolific crab apples in the front that were the source of my mother's sweet crabapple jam and apple chutney for sandwiches; a great oak for climbing; and, among others, the slim silver birch.

In my memories of that place, the weather is always fine, even when my brother and I ride our sled down the snowy lawn, a moment inevitably followed in my mind by images of colorful scarves, hats, and mittens drying on the white radiator in the bright front hall (all knitted by my mother). Otherwise, the flowerbeds are blooming and the vegetable patch is dank and rich with growth. Dark, sad things eventually happened to us in that house, but I've always had a lucky amnesia about them; a full year is lost to me, and I have little desire to retrieve it. Instead, I remember lying in bed in my very own room with its sea blue carpet, listening to the owls in the trees outside the window and feeling safe and loved.

But as a teenager, I wrote a storm sweeping that garden, and my mother a silver birch in it. I think that's actually not far wrong: firmly rooted, knowing that what it takes to survive a good buffeting is above all the ability to bend, to flex, not to brace against the wind but to ride with it. You may lose a branch or two, but you were made to endure.

I was that branch. My brother and I.

And now I obsessively peel away my mother's papery, fragile skin.

Her fearlessness took many forms. I saw it most clearly when she walked in the beech woods, alone, in the winter darkness. This was much later, when she was living in a flimsy forestry service cottage on the crest of a gentle hill—a house where I once, visiting, encountered ice in the toilet bowl. The windowsills rotted from continual condensation. Every morning she pulled on warm clothes and went out before dawn, before work, with her small terrier at her heels, no matter how it rained or the wind howled. She knew every track, every tree root and low branch; knew the dark hollows where owls dwelt or badgers kept their setts, where and when the first bluebell would most likely appear. When I stayed with her it was usually during summer holidays, when the long days meant the woods were full of light and birdsong by the time I pulled boots on with my pajamas and slipped out by the workroom door to join her, shushing the dog's excitement so my stepfather could sleep on.

Once we got a safe distance from the house and the trees closed around us, I always had so much I wanted to tell her that I found it hard to stop myself chattering, although I knew my voice was minimizing the chance we might share a rare, magical encounter with wildlife.

Occasionally I was able to visit in the darker months, when the trees were bare and no light broke the horizon until well after we were back in the kitchen again. The woods were full of movement and mysteries then: creepings, crackings, and hauntings all around. Even the dog's white patches were quickly invisible as he chased off after whatever creatures and phantoms he sensed. And there strode my mother, headscarfed and fearless. She kept her lone routine even after the dog died, although she was firm that it would be silly to get another dog now, when she was at work all day and a new pup would be nothing but extra bother and cleaning. After work and cooking, and the dishes and washing and cleaning, after keeping the household accounts and writing payment reminders to the few people who bought her husband's paintings and sculptures, the last thing she needed was another mouth to feed, another body to tend. But still she rose early for that walk, those inviolable minutes of solitude that it now became harder not to acknowledge as the one rare thing in her life that was for herself alone. Alone in the dark woods, she was never bothered.

My mother is nothing if not responsible.

From early childhood she was encouraged to bend the rules, notwithstanding her family's Methodist sobriety and the gentility they had only recently achieved. After a nervous and fragile first daughter was followed, years later, by a "miracle child," my quietly successful grandfather poured all his aspirations and support into the tomboy younger girl. He encouraged her aptitude for maths and physics, liked to share a sneaky glass of sherry with her before dinner, and turned a loving blind eye when she bunked off school to spend afternoons at the cricket— still with her schoolbooks and slide rule on her knee, jotting quick columns of figures. Her more flashy uncle took her motor racing, where the noise and the speed enthralled her, and together they tinkered on her first car, a glamorous ruin of an Austin Seven that initiated a line of impractical—and usually fast—cars that would stretch right into this, her ninth decade, before she finally grew wary of driving. She took to competitive rally driving, but in the secondary role of navigator; unlike her parents, both of whom were quite useless with maps, she and her sister were clever with spatial logic and quick thinking when circumstances required a detour. This aptitude was put to good use on many a family picnic outing, especially in the immediate postwar years when rural areas of the north of England were slow to replace the signs and waymarkers that had been removed *en masse* to confuse prospective Nazi invaders.

My timid gran worried; my mild, amused aunt (by now head girl at school, then off to a classics degree and paralyzing homesickness in London) cheered on her precocious and popular sister. My grandfather doted. When the opportunity came for my mother to pursue engineering at Cambridge, he ensured she would have whatever she needed to enjoy it to the full.

Sometimes she and my grandfather met in London for an evening, when he was down on business. They went to the newest, most fabulous restaurants—"trying them out" for his future business guests. They stayed at the Grosvenor House Hotel, a name whose slightly hushed recitation introduced glamour, for me, into any conversation in which it was mentioned. Once, she left scandalously red lipstick on his towel there. He joked for years that the hotel doorman looked at him askance forever after. It was a mild joke, an adoring one.

Her particular study was aerodynamics. Airflow over wings, through engines. Flight. She apprenticed in the same factory where Alan Turing had worked after the war—until his suicide a few years before her arrival—then got a fine job in the aircraft works that still housed, in a corner, the dusty workshop of wartime hero Barnes Wallace. (We watched *The Dambusters* a hundred times.) She was the only girl in the design lab. She wore her hair curled, pencil skirts, stilettos. She didn't really mind discovering she earned less than the men she supervised; but she did mind when the Harrier jet for which they had designed completely new propulsion systems took its first experimental flights—rising vertically from the ground like a howling specter—and each of the other members of her team got a ride in the cockpit. Insurance, she was told, covered men only. She was given a large box of chocolates.

My mother loved her work.

Of course, work ended when marriage came, to an engineer involved, as she then was, in designing the Concorde. He was in hydraulics, fluid dynamics: water to her air. Happy babies followed, and the knitting of bobble-hats and making of crabapple jam. She still attended the occasional professional conference with him—usually in a capital of the Soviet bloc: Sofia, Budapest, Prague. Places with great rivers, hill castles, cobbled streets, and modernist hotels where everyone drank cocktails and smoked. She took notes, sometimes served as translator. For evening events, she wore a fall of false hair attached to a velvet hairband that turned her short, practical fringe into the start of something much more glamorous. She wore winged eyeliner. As fascinated as I was by the hairpiece, which lived on her dressing table on a polystyrene head that my mother laughingly called "Floozy," I hated that eyeliner. My mother rarely bothered with makeup, so when she started to put it on, I knew she was going somewhere, going "Out." When I saw her at the makeup mirror, I would start crying. I begged her not to go, not to *put on the angry eyes*.

Floozy stayed behind when my mother left for good. I listened to the receding noise of the shifting gears in her shiny, teal-colored MG—the last remnant of her finery—as it gathered speed along our leafy road. I knew the sound of that engine like I knew the familiar song of a blackbird, a robin, a wren in the trees outside my bedroom or in the long, sloping back garden. Perhaps that car was the note of wild continuity between her past and the hardscrabble life she was heading into, freighted with her dying father's disappointment.

The hairpiece grew dry and tangled eventually, although I brushed it and wore it for play sometimes. It sat oddly on my wiry curls. I never saw my mother in eyeliner again, and her own hair stayed short, which was sensible. Her husband preferred it that way.

She surprised us all once more when she retired (from the last of a series of pink-collar jobs where she hid her capacity) and they promptly emigrated, leaving the hilltop cottage for a downtrodden small town in the American Deep South. It is warm and quiet—and cheap enough that they could have a house with its own swimming pool for her, and good light in the sunroom for him to make his art. In a new world, a strange culture, at an age when many people want simply whatever is familiar, she never looked back.

My mother swims every day, a few minutes of carefully preserved solitude away from the housework and her increasingly weak and querulous spouse. Her hair has turned the pure white that eventually blesses most former redheads, as straight and silky as mine is wiry and curled. It's grown long, below her shoulders; keeping it short is too much fuss. She swims on her back, mostly, slowly turning lengths, moving in and out of the shadow of the Georgia pines. She loves to watch the Mississippi kites that circle overhead on rising thermals, seeming to float on their gray wings. White hair drifts weightlessly about her face, like feathers.

Bio: *Nicola Pitchford is a British immigrant who lives in Marin County, California. She has published poetry, creative nonfiction, and literary criticism. She studied at Pomona College, the University of Wisconsin-Madison, and the 2018 Rural Writing Institute. Twitter: @NJPitchford.*

NIGHT IN DUBLIN

by Clementine E. Burnley

It is four in the morning and there is an older
man in the overstuffed blue velvet armchair by
the inglenook fireplace of the Royal Marine
Hotel in Dublin. As I retreat toward the lobby,
my book in hand, a mild resentment flares up in
me. There are other comfortable chairs dotted
around the turn-of-last-century drawing room,
but it is for the chair by the fireplace that I got
out of bed.

A plaque in the lobby announces that Laurel
and Hardy stayed here, along with Frank Sinatra,
Queen Victoria, and Charlie Chaplin. I am not
surprised. The plaque tells me I do not fit here.
Altogether the hotel is too opulent for me. My
senses have been overwhelmed by the ornate
plaster moldings, the chandeliers, the plush car-
pets, silk curtains, and streaked marble. My strict
Southern Baptist upbringing has left me with

conflicting feelings about luxury. I both yearn for the safety of wealth and am intimidated by people who have it.

I think of how this city faces the sea, like my first hometown in Cameroon. Perhaps this is why, over the years, I continue to return to Dublin, and to this hotel; to be reminded of the country I have left behind and the new one I have gained. Rich Cameroonians copy the Royal Marine style of décor, and many do it so badly I am reinforced in my belief that I am different, above the display of status through the objects I collect. No matter how hard I pretend not to long for luxury items myself, I still remember now, more than thirty years later, the car collection owned by a young man my cousin dated. I was eighteen, in Washington, DC. The young man was related to the president of Cameroon. He was always introduced as "the president's nephew," which, as West African extended families go, could have meant any degree of relatedness. At the time, his uncle had been in power for half my life. At present the president of Cameroon has been in power for thirty-nine years. Anyway, I remember the young man created a strange feeling in me. I have forgotten everything about him, but I have never forgotten my first encounter with extreme wealth. It was as if when the wings of his red Lamborghini rose above us, just by seeing them drive off in that particular car, I was also raised up into a higher mode of being.

On an impulse, I decide to walk along the road that overlooks Dublin Bay. Before I leave the hotel, I say a quick good morning to the night porter whom I read as of South Asian descent. I have not asked to satisfy my curiosity. In the week I have spent here we have become friendly but out of mutual delicacy, we do not investigate each other's ancestral genealogies.

I pull down the brim of my new cashmere hat unfashionably low, no one will see, and escape into the gale force wind. Outside, the world is different and so am I. There is silence. I enjoy the peace. I like these moments of contemplation but easily sink into morbid rumination on my racial wounds, the most dangerous of which is my longing for acceptance.

The Irish tricolor makes a blatting sound as it flaps between two European flags. I feel a real sense of sadness that is mixed with fear and anger. My country has turned away from the future those flags embody, and Ireland has embraced it. As I walk along the harbor road, I think about the gulf that has opened up between Britain, my adopted country, and the European Union. I have never gone out alone for a night walk in the decade I have lived in Berlin. Here, the sound of English has emboldened me. I feel I can be braver in my native language. Dublin seems Anglophone, Celtic, and modern. That could have been us.

For the last ten years, while I lived in Berlin, I had hoped a Europe moving toward the extreme right would be pulled back by a multicultural Britain. One of the reasons I am moving back to Britain is because I no longer feel safe in Germany. It's ironic. Racially motivated crime has risen in Britain in the two years which the rightwing press have made migrants the scapegoat for economic globalism. The target nationality changes at whim, from people of African and Asian descent, to Eastern Europeans, and then to Northern European migrants. I was shocked and then unsurprised to find out that Black British people also voted, in smaller numbers than white British people but nevertheless, people descended from migrants voted for the "Foreigners Out" parties.

A half-moon appears through a series of thin fast-moving clouds. I stop to look upward. The harbor itself is deserted when I get there. The wind plays chimes with lanyard ends against metal masts. There are wooden clatters, dull thuds against fiberglass exteriors and high notes. There are the sounds of wood on wood, and metal on metal.

I am thinking of moving back to Britain in the lee of Brexit, not because I will be safer there, but because I will be able to tell when it's time to leave Europe permanently. There is no rational reason to think my family will be safer in Britain or Ireland apart from how I feel I can read the mood better in those two places. It seems to be enough.

Migrants respond to the effects of unrestricted austerity on their countries, from which Britain has benefited since it initiated those changes in its imperial days. My Scottish lover tells me he feels safer in Berlin than in his own country on a Friday night after eleven at night when the pubs discharge an alcohol-fueled horde to ravage the high streets. I giggle.

From what I can see and feel, Celtic identity is gently marked by road signs and accent. I feel no colonial command to explain myself. It's easy to romanticize a place I only know from a luxury hotel paid for on expenses from intermittent work assignments. Still, I feel no direct threats to my body or mind here, as I often do in Germany, where white women will progress from friendly but overcurious questions before they reach out to touch my body or that of my children. I have grown used to total strangers instructing me on where my place is in the racial hierarchy. I have learned that a sentence that begins with: "I don't know what you do where you come from, but here in my country ..." will seldom end well for me. The most aggressive strangers have been men, such as the respectable left-wing liberal voter who after informing me of his voting preferences tells me, "I expect you to say good evening," when my daughter and I take the seat at a table in a restaurant where he is having dinner at a table with his wife.

People agree that, unlike the indirect Anglos and Celts, the Germans will raise uncomfortable topics. Emboldened, I mention personal experiences of racism, and the forced labor regime in place during the period of German colonial rule over Cameroon. Usually the conversation ends at that point. I have tested this out with family and left-wing friends. There is a painful disconnection afterward, no matter which words I use. In every culture there are limits to what is sayable. In Germany, the boycott of goods from Israel, and sexual abuse of children being justified as personal freedom in the left-wing intellectual circles of the 1968 movement are all off limits. Perhaps British indirectness will better match my own personal boundaries. Or perhaps after twenty years away I will miss Berlin and aspects of German directness, the way they get to the point.

"When you've a clear conscience you can sleep," an older man tells a younger man as they cross my path. We nod. Both speak a stronger accent than that which I think of as standard English, the BBC world service announcer.

A lone woman runs past. She has no eyes for me, focused on her Fitbit and I think that could be my oldest daughter, in middle England. She's the runner in our family. When I hesitate to leave the life I have built in Berlin, she asks me if I would choose for a second time to spend my life away from my immediate family. Two more women run by and their voices fade. I am fiercely glad that there are women running alone and hope they are running for themselves and not for someone else's ideas about them.

When I return to the hotel after an hour of walking in cold intermittent rain, I have not sorted the jumble of impressions in my head, but I am euphoric. I sit in a wingback chair at some distance from the fireplace and watch a live flame jump. I like the way the older man doesn't look up when I come in. He is wrapped up in his paperback. We sit in the companionship of the insomniac bibliophiles. I like his concentration, his haze of fluffy hair, pale-colored waistcoat worn under a baggy green wool jacket, and wide-legged trousers. I like the way his brown brogues tilt upward. They have molded to his feet. At seven the breakfast crowd arrives and there is no more silence. The old man and I stand up at the same time, and as we make a joint retreat toward the lifts, I decide he shares my wish to prolong the quiet. So, we do not speak.

Bio: *Clementine E. Burnley is a migrant mother, writer, and community organizer. She was longlisted for the Bridport Flash Award 2019, shortlisted for the Bristol Prize 2017, Miles Morland Award 2017, and selected for the Purple Hibiscus trust Workshop in Lagos, Nigeria in 2018. Her work appears in Emma Press' Anthology of Britain, Ink, Sweat and Tears, loss lit magazine, and Barren Magazine. You can read her work on clementine-burnley.com or find her on twitter @decolonialheart.*

THE BOOK OF OVERHEARD THINGS:

SHADOW-CATCHING AND REIMAGINING IN LOCAL POLITICS

by Elizabeth Wainwright

When I find my notebooks from yesterday, last year, last decade, I recognize myself, but she's slanted; pieces of me scattered like disco ball reflections. On this page it says, "'*Rachel, they're nice sensible shoes Rachel!'—overheard in Marks & Spencer's.*" Why did I write that down? On another page, it says: "*a girl picks up a pebble, but later discovers it's an Oystercatcher's egg.*" Most of my notebooks are full of uncategorized scribblings. The thought of other people reading them makes me uneasy. I toy with throwing them away but know I won't; they are my maps. Recently, I've started keeping a notebook for just one purpose; it's my Book of Overheard Things, and I use it to capture the words and ideas I hear in my capacity as an unexpectedly elected local politician in the UK.

I walk into a meeting in the District Council building, and I'm struck by the blandness of the room. Veneered tables try to conjure the impression of solid wood; a hot water machine intrusively boils itself; a projector and fire safety notices and hard-to-maneuver chairs fill the space. The walls are white, the floor is gray, the language is flat. Only the other councilors in the room remind me what I'm doing here. One of their faces betrays closed eyes and a tilted head. Sleep. The room lacks life. I steal a glance out the window where the trees dance and bend in the breeze, talking to each other. The center is holding, but only because it had stagnated and seized up. One whack here, one gloop of grease there, and perhaps it might move again. I've realized that whether it spirals out or, through the revelation all around us, finds a new place to turn from, is up to us.

I was once interrupted by a fellow councilor during a meeting in which we were asked to brainstorm ways to cut £1 million from our budget. I suggested we might think of ways to generate income rather than cut services. As I offered ideas, he told me to "*stop being so enthusiastic*." I wrote the words down as he continued to speak, and my Book of Overheard Things was born. He explained that we needed to be realistic. Perhaps he felt I could not hold realism and enthusiasm at the same time. But that's not my experience. The age of enlightenment, and plenty of religious thinking, has created divisions between the sacred and the secular; the sacred and the physical. How do we reconcile divided things? My experience tells me that many apparent opposites—like realism and enthusiasm—*both* have a place as we tackle local and global challenges. The poet, painter, and visionary William Blake knew that a bigger vision "*where contrarieties are equally true*" was essential, because "*without contraries is no progression*." That vision, of rejoining separated ways of being and thinking, of wholeness through individual uniqueness, is one I am trying to seek and to shape.

But that vision deflates when I find this in my Book of Overheard Things, from a senior councilor: "*My goal for my time here is to keep us solvent, and financially afloat*." That's sensible and necessary if we are to function as a local authority. And with a global pandemic, a climate in crisis, Brexit, and austerity asking too much from every direction, even that is not guaranteed. And yet I see no progress there. I want a sense of what politics *could be*. Breathing life into local politics might be one opportunity to imagine the world as it could be—one where we seek to be well known for fifteen miles, not famous for fifteen minutes; where neighborhood matters; where everyone can access dignity and well-being; where we encounter what matters and work to protect it.

Something else I noted, from a male councilor: "*I don't understand why women have so many privileges now.*" Please, go on. Because, privileges aside, I feel like I'm still struggling with some of the basics here—like being listened to and respected by some male colleagues; like being credited for my ideas (that are used by others for their gain). I'm building up the courage that I'll need to say—soon, perhaps—that I'm pregnant. That I'll plan to serve residents for as long as I can before, and as soon as I can after, giving birth. But I sense foreshadows of the reaction I might receive when I look in my notebook: "*you shouldn't have stood for election if your work means you can't attend daytime meetings.*" By that logic, the only people who stand should be retired or rich. And, in fact, the most recent census of councilors in

England by the Local Government Association showed a far higher proportion of councilors are white, male, and over sixty than in the population. Not enough women and minorities stand. The structure and process of decision-making should serve people, not the other way around. Those "many" privileges still do not give under-represented people the confidence, or time, or headspace to represent their communities and create change through politics. And so decisions are *done to* them, not for or with them, and we all suffer because of it.

I turn to my notebook and see a phrase that makes me prickle. *"You shouldn't engage the public on these [climate change] issues, it's dangerous."* Politics would be easier for many politicians if they did not have to engage with real people. But engagement is where we learn and empathize and reimagine; where I can sit down with, say, farmers and environmentalists (so often pitted against each other), and listen; where we each shift our understanding a bit. We need humility to do that. Locally, and in sub-Saharan Africa, I have seen that money and technology will not solve our challenges unless they are preceded and shaped by listening and relationship. But to engage well in the messy and exposing dance of relationship, we need the tools to do so. We need to know how to listen, how to sit with people who are not like us, who disagree with us. We need to know how to find common ground, to know things aren't as black and white as we're led to believe. Gray is a color too.

I turn back to my notebook. "*The opposition won't go after you like they do me; you're a nice young lady. You always look nice.*" I know you're trying to be kind, but you speak like I'm a wounded animal, or a doll. Please look beyond my being a "nice young lady" (I'm thirty-six and can hold my own); see my vision, my experiences; hear why the blood red soil of Devon and parts of Africa run through me; why a walk amongst trees, pulled by the scent of the evening earth, helps me find truths I can't find elsewhere. Feel my exhaustion at never being able to do enough, the disillusionment that creeps through me like a disease I'm trying to resist. Listen to the words I want to say but often don't, for fear of my hope and ideas deafening people, and of sounding immodest. Come into my mind and hear the resident imposter, always speaking. But see too how I try to overcome these things. I *am* a nice young lady, but I am also rooted as a tree and will persevere like a bird in the wind. So, *let them* go after me, if that's the only approach they know. I'd rather show them there's another way, though, beyond opposition: it involves proposition, relationship, contraries coming together, instead. But that stuff doesn't fit party politics, or win elections, yet.

Back in my notebook, and this, heard many times in many different ways: "*I've managed deals worth hundreds of millions of pounds and have made hard decisions. You may not be comfortable making hard decisions.*" You keep connecting money with discernment. Does more money make better decisions? Do you think I make bad decisions because I work with nonprofits, not banks? I'll show you places and lives affected by decisions I've made, communities thriving—and not—in faraway places because of decisions I made. My experiences help me to make hard decisions. So does listening, so does my conscience. But in my notebook: "*You can't be naïve. You must realize that you can't let your conscience guide your decisions.*"

My Book of Overheard Things helps me to catch and name the shadows. I stepped into politics conflict shy, with diminishing faith in politics as it is—but also sure that we can imagine and create a better politics and so a better world using low-tech ingredients we already have; strong in the everlasting hope that one day the root of the word conscience—the faculty of knowing what is right; a sense of justice; a moral sense—might be the *only* thing that guides us in our decisions.

Bio: *Elizabeth Wainwright is an elected District Councilor, a writer, and a coach & mentor for individuals and organizations. She has lived and worked around the world, particularly across sub-Saharan Africa, and she led the development of an international community development charity called Arukah Network. She is based in Devon, in the South West UK, and enjoys getting out to its coastlines and to Dartmoor National Park. She was selected to be part of the Inaugural Rural Writing Institute and is (slowly) working on a book. Learn more at www.ElizabethJWainwright.com and follow Elizabeth on Twitter @LizWainwright.*

NON-TRADITIONAL

by Rebecca White

I remember the first time I realized not all dads went to prison. I must have been around nine years old. A conversation with school friends in the playground; my friend Jasmine's jokey comment; the penny finally dropping. Years later, a similar revelatory moment while watching Australian soap opera *Home & Away* (I'm aware of the bathos). A domestic violence storyline. She shouldn't have provoked him. Did you hear how spiteful she was? He doesn't know any better. It's only because he was drunk. And insecure. And damaged. My boyfriend's casual reply: "Does your dad hit your mum or something?".

Slowly—far too slowly—I came to realize that my working-class background wasn't just that. Sure, it was working class, but with a hefty dose of dysfunction and trauma. I've never connected with the idea of being proud of what you were born into—your country, your town, your class. For me, that road leads to all sorts of –isms that I strive to stand up against. Patriotism, jingoism, nationalism, classism, racism, ableism, sexism. Superiorism. How can I be proud of something I had no part in? Can you be proud of winning the lottery—or losing?

But while I'm not proud of identifying as working class, I am passionate about it. "*Classism: prejudice or discrimination against people belonging to a particular social class.*" That's always been my very own chip on my shoulder. Something I spent over twenty years trying to remove. The feeling of injustice, of never quite fitting in. Until another penny dropped. That chip on my shoulder is still there because the discrimination and inequality is still there.

When I went to a prestigious London university at eighteen, I quit after one semester. I loved my subject (French and Hispanic studies). My grades were more than good enough—but was my background? The culture shock of entering an elite institution, my new home ushering in "the best years of my life," was brutal and unexpected. Exchanges with fellow students were peppered with markers that let me know just how different I was—parents' professions and alma maters, unpaid internships, holiday homes, gap years volunteering, and lunchtime shopping trips to Selfridges. These teenagers exuded intangible and unquantifiable qualities I didn't know I was missing, precisely because I wasn't familiar with them: quiet confidence, self-assuredness, a sense of being comfortable in your own skin. I felt like I didn't fit in precisely because I didn't. It took me a year to muster up the conviction to restart my degree at a different (slightly less elite) university.

I was a strong student. But when it came to considering postgraduate study in my field, a quick cost-benefit analysis confirmed and justified my core beliefs. People like me don't take risks like that. There could never be a return on the financial investment. No guaranteed lucrative career path, no generational wealth to fall back on. My friends were surprised, and blind to the privilege that made them so.

Fifteen years on, one of the many doors I'd been knocking on for so long opened. I finally managed to move into the field where my heart lies: social justice. I now work at a large human rights organization. The underrepresentation of the working class, or those from lower socioeconomic backgrounds, is stark and yet largely unseen. The barriers to accessing and flourishing in these spaces, even as a white, able-bodied, cisgender, heterosexual woman, are manifold. Look at this whole situation through an intersectional lens and weep.

My bachelor's degree and years of unpaid volunteering alongside a full-time job managed to secure what is essentially an entry-level role. I've not once had to use my foreign language skills, despite them being a prerequisite for interview. I'm the only one in my office without a master's degree. These hiring practices and organizational policies are unintentionally exclusionary—designed by the people already in these organizations for the kind of people already in these organizations. During water cooler moments and after-work drinks, those verbal markers of privilege are still there. Same but different. The housing ladder, nannies, cleaners, further study. Options. Where are the other women who identify as working class? Have they code-switched and assimilated to the point that I can't see them, or is it, as I suspect, that they're just not there?

With motherhood came more barriers to navigate in the workplace alongside my imposter syndrome. My "matresence" kick-started a profound change in identity; once again I found myself scrabbling to find my place in the world. Add to that my desire—my need—to be the mother to my children that I didn't have. My hypervigilance regarding my children's emotional well-being, coupled with financial and logistical restraints, has led to me taking part-time jobs where every other sentence is a "just" or an "only." My search criteria is based on commute times and flexible working policies. Once again, that feeling of surprise at realizing how differently my middle-class colleagues experience parenthood. The concomitant envy—understated but ever present.

A few months ago, I was invited to speak at a girls' school in a deprived area of London. Part of a widening participation initiative, I was to talk about the benefits of pursuing traditional academic subjects. These were potential first-generation university students—predominantly Black and Asian—who were interested in vocational courses that led to a clear career path. And then there's me, council-estate girl made good. How could I tell them to follow their hearts and academic calling knowing the obstacles they'd face? Knowing their student debt would be five times more than mine ever was? That qualifications from BAME people were not valued as much as their white counterparts'?[1]

How could I inspire them by divulging that, to access the not-for-profit sector for example, they'd have to do a master's degree and various internships or volunteer roles to finally land an entry-level job on a mediocre salary? That, after all that, they would probably encounter racism, classism, and sexism in the sector whose ultimate aim is to combat inequality? I couldn't. I couldn't admit that I feel betrayed by the system and foolish for thinking my career could align with my idealistic vision of a more just world. What I could tell them, with all sincerity, was that their voices are important. Now more than ever. In an increasingly unequal society which has fallen hard for the myth of meritocracy, their voices need to be heard.

Recently, the concept of "lived experience" has gained traction. Organizations extol the value of "experts by lived experience." In other words, ordinary people. People who have practical and not solely theoretical experience of certain realities and identities,

---

1 Nearly 40 percent of Black African graduates are in non-graduate jobs—nearly double the White British rate of 20 percent (Runnymede Trust).

who have gone through ordinary, sometimes extraordinary, things. People who are LGB-TQI+, migrants, not white, Gypsy, Roma, Traveler, younger, older, disabled, working class, "survivors" (of conflict, trauma, abuse, illness …). People outside of the homogenous group that most of these organizations comprise. Academia, government, civil society—in order to have any legitimacy, these sectors need to include the very people they claim to represent.

But who does this diversity really benefit? Tokenism can be more harmful than invisibility. Underrepresented groups don't need to be "empowered," no matter how well intentioned. For this implies the power is still in the hands of those maintaining the status quo. What's needed is the space to assert their own power, for the greater good.

My use of the third person when referring to underrepresented groups is not so much deliberate as instinctive. Would my "lived experience" (or "life," as I like to call it) be of genuine value to my employers? My working-class reality isn't a badge of honor for me—this "expertise" doesn't provide an opportunity to tap into a target demographic, nor is it something to draw on in a workshop. My suburban community wasn't close-knit; it was soulless and divided. My neighbors were not "salt of the earth," they were racist and judgmental. My dad loved hard, worked hard, and drank hard—until he left. My mum was depressed; too focused on her own emotional survival to consider mine. I remember her actively discouraging me from going back to university after I dropped out first time round— "Ah, Rebecca, the more you learn, the less you seem to earn." I didn't get a degree because of parents, but in spite of them.

It's this double aspect of my identity that I struggle to own. I bring my values to work with me every single day, but not my whole self. I try to highlight and tackle the under-representation of "minoritized" people in the organizations where I work and volunteer, but not from the vantage point of "lived experience." I don't talk about the racism and homophobia I grew up around, or the criminality, debt, and violence within my family. I choose not to disclose. A product of a society and a family where women are told that appearance is everything. Don't answer back; cover up the bruises. Bear other people's anger but never unleash your own. Yes, I stay silent; but I do the work. Sadly, and wholeheartedly. With that invisible chip on my shoulder which isn't going anywhere. That chip is my fire.

"You cannot use someone else's fire. You can only use your own. And in order to do that, you must first be willing to believe that you have it." —Audre Lorde

Bio: *Rebecca lives in London, UK, where she was born and bred. Her politics is personal, her feminism is intersectional. She's also a mum to two wonderful little critical thinkers.*

HIDE-AND-SEEK

by Sara Collie

The year I graduated from university and took my first tentative steps into adulthood, my grandpa died. The day after his funeral, as we were clearing out the house he had lived in for over sixty years, I found my grandmother there, unexpectedly, playing hide-and-seek.

It was unexpected because she had been dead for about ten years. Present only as an absence in our lives, looming large around the edges. Grandpa had long since forgotten she had died: he had spent the last few years looking for her in all the wrong places and faces, finding her mistakenly in my mother, and later in me. He would say her name uncertainly as he looked at us, and we would shake our heads quietly. "No, she's gone, remember?" But dementia had clouded his eyes and blurred his memory. He was adamant she was around somewhere, perhaps outside in the garden?

But as it turned out, Grandma was there in the front room all along, hiding in three different cupboards, chopped up, waiting for me like a jigsaw puzzle with missing parts. I have taken years to try to put the pieces back together, hoping to discover something about who she was and where I come from, so that I might have a better idea of who I really am. But it has turned into an increasingly urgent game of hide-and-seek where all the rules have changed: I find her and then she's gone again, my memory as muddled as Grandpa's in those last years, despite the fact that I am now in my thirties and otherwise completely *compus mentis*.

The first piece I found was in a small corner cupboard. I opened the door to check if anything was inside, and there she was. The smell of her was unmistakable: pressed powder and just the faintest hint of cigarettes. She had always kept her makeup there; as a young girl I would watch with fascination as she reached up and took it down, beginning the well-rehearsed routine of applying foundation, patting it into her wrinkled face in small efficient motions. The blusher would be next, and then she would outline her lips perfectly in pale pink, coloring the lines in with matching lipstick. My grandma was not a vain lady, nor did she have many occasions to dress up, living as she did in a small, rural village all her life, and yet every day she would sit and make up her face. I opened up the compact to find the round sponge still there in the concave circle of powder. The small mirror inside the lid was coated with powdery dust, but one sharp breath cleared the glass. Last time anybody had looked into it, it was her face that looked out. Now it was just my own features staring back at me. Where had she gone?

The second place I found her was in the cupboard under the stairs. A skeleton in the closet, but not the scary kind, just the very bones of her, the structures on which everything hung. There in the murk and dust, behind boxes and an old vacuum cleaner, one of her old paintings had been tucked away and forgotten about. It was unframed, painted directly onto a piece of old board. A vibrant landscape of the garden, done from the back of the house, looking down the path that led through lawns and borders, between hedges, past the coal shed, all the way to the huge, hidden vegetable patch at the end. The painting captures the scene more accurately than any photo ever taken, but what I really see when I look at it is her. She is there in every careful brushstroke, in every colorful smudge of red begonias and towering foxgloves, in the dappled mass of lilac blooms. She was that garden: the garden was her. She knew every plant like an old friend, knew instinctively how to nurture everything that grew there, making it come to life, just like the painting. I carried her home and dusted her off carefully. I have propped the painting up everywhere I have lived in the ten years since. It is still unframed; I cannot quite get past the idea that placing glass over it might suffocate her.

That my grandmother should appear to me as a makeup compact and an old painting was no great surprise: transformation was her specialty. I was still very small when she taught me how to press a seed into the ground where it could become something so much bigger. By the next time I visited, it would be a towering vine, the tips bursting with small red flowers. The time after that it would have been transformed into the food on my plate: runner beans served hot and steaming as part of an almost entirely homegrown Sunday lunch. She showed me how to rub fat and flour together too, so that it made "breadcrumbs," which, when mixed with milk, would become a ball of pastry that we would roll out and drape over a pie pan filled with raspberries that we had picked together. This would be brushed with egg, sprinkled with sugar, and alchemized into a crust of fine, golden pastry in the Aga. We would eat these meals together as a family around the table in the front room. When the eating was done, I would take her lessons about transformation and make them my own, sliding out of my seat into the other dimension that existed under the table, shut off from the rest of the world by the colorful gingham tablecloths that dangled to the floor. In that place full of feet and shoes and the swish of skirts and trouser legs where adults' voices were nothing more than a dull, faraway murmur, I would use the gifts she gave me: imagination, wonder, self-sufficiency. I was a little too old for playing under the table by the time she died, but I did not lose the sense of how powerful that little old lady was, even though she had been visibly shrinking for years. I did not forget how she could transform just about anything into something better with a sleight of hand. An old board, a patch of land, flour, fat, family.

Her third incarnation was inside a large bureau opposite the fireplace. The day we were there to clear the house, I found her in the pages of a small pocketbook diary. It was not the grandma I recognized from memories or family stories. In it, she had a different face, one that bore a sadder, darker expression. One that I had never seen until that day. Perhaps that was what the makeup was for? All the better to hide herself with?

The diary was the kind with one week per double-page spread and flimsy pages rimmed in gold. The frontispiece was a list of facts: her name, address, and date of birth, all neatly copied out in careful hand. Other than that, most weeks were left blank, rare appointments noted, special dates ringed and marked with our names and respective ages. Everything else she wrote—fewer words than fill this page— were something akin to an almanac, charting weather systems that rolled in and out, the turning of the tides both high and low; an attempt to somehow note and know the dark shores she was venturing in. I had known nothing of her skills in this field. I had known nothing of the fear I felt in those pages.

It went like this: Grandpa's initial or name in shortened form and simple words like "very dark mood" or "bad again" with arrows extending either side to designate the duration of the pressure systems that were darkening her horizons, before "better now" or "back to normal" (whatever normal was). A careful, almost-code for awful truths; days, weeks of shifting sands, a charting of the climate in their house. Every storm that rumbled through, each one marked in black or blue.

These atmospheres, we knew them too, their astronomical proportions: how he'd take a hammer to anything he couldn't fix and smash it instead, or else dwell darkly at the edges of things, seeping his seething silences over all occasions. But we hardly ever spoke of it, and certainly not about what it was like for her. We stuck to the nicer narrative about how much they loved each other: the ballroom dancing trophies they had won lined up on the mantelpiece; how sad and broken he was when she died, how all he wanted was to find her again. Of course, he loved her, of course. But that wasn't the whole picture.

Holding her that day in my shaking hands, I did not know what to do with her, with those dusty, desolate pages. Unlike the compact mirror, unlike the painting, I could not wipe her clean this time. It would have smudged the ink, ripped the pages, muddied the truth. We had all helped to sweep that dust under the carpet with our silence in the face of Grandpa's unfathomable moods and she had carefully, furtively, gathered it in the cracks of those gold-rimmed pages. A trail of dust, like breadcrumbs leading back, the territory neatly mapped and laid out bare for all to see. But it was too late. I showed the diary to my auntie, watched a small, careful frown form on her forehead, saw the sadness glaze her eyes. She knew all about the spaces between the arrows, that much I am certain of. If we talked about it, I don't remember. My memory is hazy, like the version of my grandma that I found that day in the writing cupboard.

The game of hide-and-seek that started that day has been going on ever since, the rules mutating and shifting as time passes by. I don't know quite who I am looking for anymore or how much—if anything—is still hidden from me. Quite how bad were the days between the arrows? Was it just dark moods, or was it words, actions, violence? Was the makeup she put on a careful mask, or was it really war paint? Was she so good at transforming things because that was the only way to be there in that house with him? To take something bad and make it better, with sleight of hand, all the while hiding there in those coded notes. Why the mystery? Should I hide too? The vague threat that lingers around these questions had me convinced that that was the only safe thing to do for years. She said so much in so few words. I can only say so little. But I don't want either of us to end up in pieces, hidden in cupboards, transformed into a cryptic code, unseen, discarded, gathering dust.

All I can be certain of is that there is so much I don't know about who she was or who my grandpa really was, or who anybody in my family is, myself included. And even though I've spent the last decade and a half trying to work it out, there are still gaps, blind spots, secrets, and things I cannot know. All I can do is dab words onto a page, like pressed powder, like paint, like egg on pastry crust, like arrows and initials on flimsy pages, and cross my fingers and hope against hope that I have just a fraction of the power to create and transform that she did. That somehow, I will turn this mass of words into a me that I can look in the face and maybe find her there again, looking back out at me, much more complicated than I remember her being as a child. And so much more powerful.

Ready or not, here I come.

Bio: *Sara Collie is a writer, teacher and wandering soul living in Cambridge, England. Her writing explores the wild, uncertain spaces of nature, the ups and downs of mental health, and the mysteries of the creative process. She has a Ph.D. in Contemporary French Literature and her poetry and prose have appeared in various journals and anthologies. She is currently writing a memoir about her experiences hiking across the Pyrenees.*

THE REST IS POETRY:

WHY WE COME OUT

by Sonja Franeta

In Buenos Aires, the women sat in a circle
called by an older woman, a writer and activ-
ist. In her sixties and just joyfully out as a les-
bian, it was Ilse who convened this gathering
of women-loving women. She suggested that
all of them write down stories of their loves,
without signing their names. They did so. She
collected the stories, shuffled them, and dealt
them out again like a pack of cards. She asked
one woman to read aloud the story she had
been dealt. "I fell in love with the mother of
my child's friend." There was quiet. Another
read the story she had randomly received: "I
went to church and confessed after kissing a
girl the first time. Although I felt guilty, I did it
again, and I no longer confessed and stopped

going to church altogether." Then another
and another. Such amazing and engaging
stories. Spontaneously, one of the women,
Amelia, proudly claimed hers was the one
just read. More stories were read; more were
claimed. In the end, all the women identified
with their respective remarkable, beautiful,
and fantastic stories.

The desire to make public what is most private
is what moved me to collect and publish inter-
views of queers in Russia. Over a period of time
in the 1990s, I collected coming-out stories of
men and women in Russia. Sometimes these
interviews chronicled moments when individu-
als thought about their coming out as an event
for the first time. Some interviewees felt trans-
formed by the interview itself.

Making public what is feared, risking ridicule
or castigation, is a demanding undertaking—a
decisive step in favor of life. For the interviewer
and translator it involves even more—under-
standing words and intonations, working with
people in the whirlwind of their own individual
and national histories, and also making many
choices about how to publish the material.
Complicating matters are family problems, the
politics of a country (repressive laws), differing

cultural understandings (butch/femme or other gender roles), and much more.

In the course of my work I shared some of my own writings and erotic poetry with the Russians I met. In a sense, I was coming out over and over with people I was meeting there. I wanted them to experience this openness.

In Moscow, my friend Lena said to me one day in 1992, "It is puzzling to me that you feel the need to describe some of the most intimate details of sexual desire in your poetry. It doesn't seem like you are the one writing the poetry; it's as if the poetry comes from a different person." That person was indeed me, intimate, erotic details notwithstanding.

While Lena had been living with her woman partner for over twenty years, it was difficult for her (and others) to identify in any way with the label lesbian. I got the feeling that they had never even uttered the word before I met them. Over time, as Lena became an activist, that changed.

Who is to judge whether reluctance to talk about one's sexuality is a genuine need for privacy, a form of internalized homophobia, or historical legacy? In my explorations, I am becoming aware of how slow and varied the process is. It is worth representing this aspect of human life—the history and customs of a people. Do I personally have a right to write about all this? Should I be publishing a book of interviews with people telling me about their most intimate stories and hidden lives? I felt it was my interviewees who took the step and gave me permission to make their stories public.

I have come to understand this question better during my incredible journey with my Russian friends. When I listen to them, I comprehend parts of my own sexual history and family and social dynamics. I too become more public. What is generally considered very private even in US society is made public so that sexual minorities can be liberated. Gays and lesbians have been forced to be secretive about our sexuality to survive. To counteract homophobia, we reveal our same-sex orientation in our art and activism, in the way we dress, and finally in coming out. This is the beginning of our freedom. In the US, the act of coming out reached full force in the 1970s and 1980s as a movement of pride and celebration.

In 1992, I was struck by Lena's observation, yet I didn't know if it was just another case of homophobia or simply that she had never read lesbian erotica in poetry before. There had been no gay movement in Russia. They never were exposed to the wealth of literature and music that had already been produced and unearthed by the queer movement in the US. It was all new to my friend, and it took time for her to take it in.

I remembered how fiercely I had to repress my sexuality as I grew up—my shame about the feelings, the glimmers of attraction to several girlfriends. They were much more intense than my feelings for boys. To my friend, Mary, I wrote impassioned letters in my preteen and early teen years, expressing "my care and concern for you, my confusion about what I feel, even my undying love." To my friend Celia, a little later, as a sixteen-year-old, I wrote a poem about a rose who wanted so much to be picked, the thorns were dangerous, the beauty precious.

At the time, I firmly pushed away any thought of physical closeness no matter how strong the urges. I didn't want to risk being rejected or sneered at. I had heard the word lesbian, and it was trampled on. I relegated the word to the bad pile, but what was so great about relating to boys? They didn't relate to me, and they seemed to be a lot of trouble. Boys were aggressive, strange because of their odd sexual needs, and they didn't seem to be interested in me.

One of the first times I felt a real physical attraction for another girl was for Celia. She sometimes spent the night at my home in the Bronx. My mother would set up a separate cot alongside my own bed for her. Celia had just put on her nightgown and I felt very conscious of her body, her large frame, the rise and fall of her breasts as she breathed several feet away from me. She was staring at me and I at her. She looked beautiful to me, because I loved her and our friendship felt good. Something very powerful—a sudden beam of light, the reverberation of a cello, the wash of an unexpected wave—passed between us. Our gazes became one gaze, as Shakespeare or another poet had noted centuries ago. Yet we were girls, the same sex, nothing good could come of these intense feelings.

I wanted to be close to her—physically. She asked me to hug her. I went to her, pushing the feeling of queerness away. I felt her chest move against mine. I wanted to hold her much longer, but I quashed my desire and we separated. I wonder what she thought as we went to our separate beds. I remember looking at her and finding yearning in her eyes, even in the half-light of my small room. In my bed I turned away from her gaze after saying goodnight. I turned away from her, fighting my desires, feeling exhausted.

It was not until the mid-seventies while on a trip to Soviet Russia, away from my husband, my family of origin, and US society, that I felt drawn to a particular woman again. We were walking by the river in Narva, and questions of life and identity came up.

"Did you ever think about relating to a woman?" my new friend Gina asked, knowing I was married. I was so shocked I could barely answer her. Tears came to my eyes. I had already felt an attraction to her, but it was still unspeakable for me.

I began to free myself from the repression, this denial of my self. As we spoke from the heart about our lives and our observations, I felt a growing kinship with her and a trust in what I was feeling, an irresistible attraction I could no longer ignore or deny. That night, alone in a room we shared in Estonia, my feelings rose to the surface. As we continued to talk from our beds even after saying goodnight, I could no longer keep myself in check. There was no reason to, here in Estonia, far away from everything. I told myself that if Gina said one more word I would go to her. I did.

"I just want to hug you," I pleaded. She blinked at me and after a moment took me in, encircling me with her arms. I embraced her, feeling a release I had never felt before. My breath was deep, as if I were blowing on a wind instrument. I felt her skin against mine, the smoothness of it, her smell, the softness of her breasts and my own—unforgettable. I unlocked years of pent-up feelings. Dreams became possible.

I became me.

The rest is poetry.

Coming out is poetry.

Bio: *Sonja Franeta is a writer, educator, translator, and activist born in the Bronx to an immigrant Yugoslav family. In 2004, she published ten interviews of Siberian queers, Rozovye Flamingo, in the original Russian, in collaboration with friends at the LGBT Archives in Moscow. In 2017, Sonja Franeta's English translation became available—Pink Flamingos: 10 Siberian Interviews. Her collection, My Pink Road to Russia: Tales of Amazons, Peasants and Queers, came out in 2015 and is now translated into Russian too. She divides her time between St. Petersburg Florida and Northern Spain with her partner Sue and their two cats.*

DISABLING NARRATIVES

by Amy Kenny

Every comic book villain from Ulysses Klaue (*Black Panther*) to Mr. Glass (*Unbreakable*) to Dr. Poison and Ares/Sir Patrick Morgan (*Wonder Woman*) teaches us that superheroes are not the ones with disabilities. Even Darth Vader's dissent to the Dark Side coincides with his disfigurement. Disability is to be feared, ostracized, villainized. It becomes an external manifestation of some inner malevolence. Ultimately, the hero defeats the character with the disability and restores normative order to the world. Insert collective sigh of relief. Everyone left is able-bodied, and therefore moral.

When we finally receive a portrayal of disability that is not conflated with evil, it is generally depicted by an able-bodied actor putting on disability like a costume for an academy award. As if our bodies are props that can be used for accolades but quickly discarded when they become too heavy, too spontaneous, too messy. Disability cannot be reconstructed via empathy cosplay. You can't use a wheelchair for an afternoon and understand what my life is like. Our language is no better. People co-opt the experience of disability as a metaphor to explain exhaustion and limitation. Like a poor night's sleep can make you understand what it feels like for an incident to be truly "paralyzing" or "crippling." As if you know what it's like to be "lame" or "crazy" or "blind" to something.

Disabled characters are metaphors, and little else. They are repositories for able-bodied fears about becoming disabled. They do not possess multifaceted personalities that exist in the real world. They become empty receptacles on which able-bodied writers project their pity, as though people with disabilities are objects of suffering instead of subjects with unique personalities and gifts. Disability must always serve a loftier "purpose" that drives narrative closure, instead of simply existing as an aspect of diverse humanity. Generally speaking, there are limited acceptable roles for disabled characters in movies, pop culture, and society:

1. **Archetype:** Villainous disabled nemesis
   Qualities: Melancholic angst, dejected re-
   sentment, he's got an ax to grind with the
   world because of his unfair lot in life (read:
   he's disabled after all!)
   Catchphrase: "Let the hate flow through
   you" or "we stop looking for monsters under
   our bed when we realize they're inside us"
   Purpose: Disability acts as both cause and
   symptom of his comic book villainy, but it
   doesn't need to be explained because every-
   one naturally assumes he is angry at the
   world. His disability is usually acquired, not
   congenital, so it can serve as the only detail
   given from his tragic backstory.

2. **Archetype:** Virtuous disabled overcomer
   Qualities: Abundant patience, winsome
   attitude, saccharine smile
   Catchphrase: "Everything happens for
   a reason" or "the only disability is a bad
   attitude"
   Purpose: She'll serve as your inspiration
   so you can overcome the trivial difficulty
   of your sprained ankle or overdemanding
   boss. She inspires you to do everything with

a smile, because she's the epitome of the person who has it "worse off." Her personality is almost entirely undetectable, except when you need someone to compete with in oppression Olympics.

Most narratives teach us that characters with disabilities demand some kind of narrative termination. Cure or kill them off. As if all we needed was an emboldening "Run, Forrest, run!" or a revenge plot to cast off our coma-induced disability and escape to freedom.[1] Disability has already served its function and therefore can be discarded. Phew!

To live with a disability, then, is to live a life of erasure. There is no space for us to live fully embodied lives outside of offering inspiration porn in able-bodied narratives. Sure, we are box office gold when we "overcome" our physical limitations or maintain an optimistic attitude during diagnoses that everyone openly dreads. The roles for people with disabilities are pre-scripted to ensure able-bodied people feel noble about themselves, as if our entire existence is in service to their emotional journeys.

---

1 I reference *Forrest Gump* and *Kill Bill* here, but throwing off a disability is a well-documented trope.

The project of disabled womanhood is to slowly, almost imperceptibly, give up tiny pieces of yourself, until one day, there is none of you left, except what everyone else projects onto you. A disabled woman is scripted to be a mirror, reflecting an image of inspirational selflessness back to others, showcasing everyone else's best traits, instead of revealing any of her own grit. We are taught from these narratives that our lives are not worth living, that most people would kill themselves if they had what we had. We are taught that we should hide our pain; that with enough pills, we can numb it or at the very least, distract ourselves from it. We are taught to conceal it from everyone else, as if our disability will disappear if we just perform normalcy dipped in mawkish smiles. We are taught that our wayward bodies make people uncomfortable, as if someone else's perceived distress is more important than our own. We are told to swallow our feelings for the sake of centering another's consolation, never questioning the emotional tax of embodying a feigned persona. (Reader, I have heard all of these horrors directly to my face. *Imagine what they say behind my back.*)

I used to play the game. I thought if I could just perform a veneer of perfection, it would inoculate me from their patronizing taunts and invasive interrogations about my body. I believed that I could perfect my way out of people demeaning disability, that somehow my fastidiousness would endow me with dignity in their eyes. But all it did was put me on a carousel of dehumanization and made me feel complicit in their rhetorical violence against people with disabilities.

To let someone in on my (sometimes-invisible) disability is an intimate and vulnerable act. *Will they believe me? Will they pity me once they know? Will their ableism overshadow their opinion of me?* I have the privilege of choosing when to involve someone in my disability.

Until I don't.

To live with my disability is to constantly move back and forth between my two selves: one that appears able-bodied and independent, and one that is (noticeably) disabled and interdependent. People only ever see one version of me, but I am both and neither in every moment, converging in the warp of Crip time.[2] Whenever I walk with a cane or use my wheel-

---

2 Crip time is a way of thinking about how people with disabilities experience time in a non-linear way. See https://dsq-sds.org/article/view/5824/4684.

chair, I unwittingly perpetuate the notion that disability must be performed in order to be validated. My mobility scooter (named "Diana, Princess of the My-scooter"), my electric blue cane, my stumbling gait all proclaim my disability to the world, inviting a scrutinizing gaze that casts my body as public property. "Sleep with soap," she endorses. "Bathe with Epsom salt," he recommends. "Have you tried rubbing herbs on your feet? It helped my cousin ..." They trail off. The hubris of offering remedies to someone with a disability derives from these reductive kill-or-cure narratives. I am not a character in *that* story. I do not get to throw off my disability in a poignant crescendo to make audiences feel better about themselves.

There is no available narrative that fits my disability. It is visible and invisible, public and private, existing in the liminal space of Crip reality. When I am walking unassisted, my disability lurks beneath like muscle memory of another life. My eyes relentlessly look up because I know what it's like to experience the world from below, sitting in my chair. When I use my mobility scooter, I know the movements that my legs can no longer make. *Heel, toe, heel toe, heel, toe.* My body keeps score even when no one else registers my disability. *Only do 80 percent or you won't be able to get dressed by yourself tomorrow.* My body exists in no narrative, because it is complex, nuanced, and messy, and does not offer neat resolution.

What remains largely invisible in these narratives is the assumed able-bodiedness of society, an identity that lingers without scrutiny. People who are able-bodied are generally unaware of their own embodiment in the way that people with disabilities are. Able-bodies masquerade as normative and therefore become the uninterrogated default. Most able-bodied people I know are blithely unaware of how the social construct of disability contributed to their own mythos of selfhood. They have not asked themselves questions about the limitations of their body because it has always been an assumed, reliable norm. They do not have to imagine the lyricism of their limbs because they are dependable, consistent, steadfast.

Until they aren't.

By either age or accident, most people will experience some form of disability at some point in their lives. Disability knows no time, gender, race, ethnicity, or class. It eventually encounters us all. Those of us who have already lived in its company know how to welcome it. Those of us who are already marked by it know how to rewrite its histories from the liminal space of our bodies.

We need a new language of embodiment that is not coated in the residue of ableism. We need to tell new stories about disability that allow us to exist without serving a narrative purpose. Even the demand for narrative closure is inherently ableist. Disability is ...

Bio: *Amy Kenny holds a PhD in early modern literature and culture and has published articles on dramaturgy, performance of laughter, the senses, and diseases in Shakespeare's plays, and a monograph entitled Humoral Wombs on the Shakespearean Stage. She is disabled and invested in the work of disability justice.*

AN INCONVENIENCE

by Sandra Corbett

I have epilepsy. Officially diagnosed at the age of thirteen, I had experienced odd feelings in my head and blackouts for years. After several appointments with neurologists, I was told I had epilepsy in the form of absence seizures. I experienced these absences for the first sixteen years of my life. These were then replaced for an unknown reason by tonic-clonic seizures, which I currently have. This is the convulsive epilepsy that most people think of when they think of the condition. I personally would never describe myself or anyone else as an "epileptic." It automatically places a point of difference between another person and me. We are all people, and I have striven to not be so different that others might consider me an inconvenience.

This part of my life started on a family holiday. I was eight years old, and I was tired. This living room was fun for an eight-year-old, as it had a rocking chair, and I apparently rocked myself unconscious. My parents first thought I was just being a brat and not answering them, but as it became apparent that I wasn't conscious, my father ran to the house next door to get the number of a doctor. I woke up the next afternoon approximately twelve hours later, in a bed that wasn't mine and wearing my mum's nightshirt. I have never spoken to my family about this, and I can only imagine how upsetting and terrifying it must have been for them to have their child go unconscious for no apparent reason. I was still undiagnosed; therefore, schools I attended did not know there was anything they should have on their record or have staff be trained for. When I was twelve years old, I had a fit in my school swimming pool. We were having a lesson and of course no one knew there was anything wrong with me until I was asked what was wrong. I was physically unable to answer with my head spinning out of control and a paralyzing sensation between my brain and my vocal cords. I was escorted from the swimming pool by the headmaster and walked down the communal hallway in my swimming costume. I am appalled for myself as a twelve-year-old when I think of this image.

Of course, the staff only had my best interests at heart and were worried. I cannot really describe what it was like. I get emotional when I think about my past experiences talking about epilepsy, even if it is one sentence. I do tell myself I am absolutely fine with it, but it is only occasionally that I am.

People's ignorance from time to time amazes me. This generally comes by them not realizing they've said anything insensitive. I once recorded a documentary about epilepsy, which I really enjoyed. It was relaxed, and it brought light to an audience that may not have known much about epilepsy otherwise. On the first day of filming, the director asked if he could continue filming if I were to have a fit. Writing this makes me cry, because I said yes. I did not want to be an inconvenience to him. It sounds ridiculous. It is ridiculous.

Once at school, a group of people didn't want to do a gym class. A friend of mine said, "It's fine. Sandra can just faint and we won't have to do anything." I laughed, of course. If you do not laugh, you are thought of as not being able to take a joke. Inside, of course, I wanted to cry.

On another occasion, I was at dinner with a friend and she asked, "Do you piss yourself?" I am grateful and understand people wanting to know what to do and what could happen if I were to have a fit. Whether I pee or not makes no difference to anyone. I have a strange and persistent inability to confront people when they make even the most unknowingly insensitive comment, and I imagine other people with epilepsy may feel the same.

Throughout my childhood until I left for university, every time I were to go to the shower and a shampoo bottle fell over, my mother would shout and ask if I was okay. Eventually when things fell in the shower, I would just yell that I was okay. It was a strange norm. I tend to tell new friends that I have epilepsy in general conversation. In my head, if I seem fine about it, psychologically I hope they realize there is no reason for them to panic. The most common question I get asked in a situation like this is, "What should I do if it happens?" This is an excellent and relieving question to hear, and I am always thrilled to answer it—it shows they care and are willing to help me should the worst happen.

I have been on medication since I was thirteen years old. My mother used to go to appointments with neurologists because I was so young. I have been on several different types of medication, but the first was known to damage a fetus in the womb and was therefore advised against for pregnant women with epilepsy. My neurologist asked if I was planning to start a family any time soon at the age of thirteen. I understand procedure, but I also understand stupidity in situations. I have gone through exceptional low points, considering my worth as a result of this inconvenience inside me. This is a side effect of medication, or perhaps it is just something that everyone thinks about from time to time.

Despite having epilepsy, I do not feel it has hindered me in any way regarding opportunity. I have traveled solo and have done for years. I have two university degrees. I am not saying this as if I am any better for having gone through university. I am only hoping to show that it should not stop people with epilepsy considering projects and options. I have never been able to drive. This tends to be the main topic of conversation whenever I see extended family. "Have you learned to drive yet?" "No. The bus is fine." "It's very useful to have." I have always been amazed at how another person's ability or non-ability to drive is of such interest to another. I couldn't care less if anyone could or could not drive and certainly would not bring it up in conversation, particularly persistently! Who cares!

So, who cares? Plenty people, from my friends and family to health professionals. I realize I come with this inconvenience from a place of immense privilege. I am a Scottish citizen with access to the National Health Service as and when I need it. If I have a problem, or even a question, my neurologist is more than happy to help me. I know I have the strongest support system in family and friends. Not everyone has that, as they live their lives with their own inconveniences.

Bio: *Sandra Corbett graduated from The University of Edinburgh with an M.A. (Hons) French and Spanish followed by an MLitt Publishing Studies from the University of Stirling. She has worked in the National Library of Scotland, in the media and is currently working in publishing.*

HOW IT FEELS TO
BE BROKEN

by Shenai Moore

The morning is cold and gray, the sky spitting raindrops and tiny shards of ice. My son, Grayson, and I sit shivering in the car as we wait for the heater to wake up and do its job. The excitement in the car is palpable. As I shift into reverse, a text chimes through.

"I can't do this. God wants me to keep my baby. Please don't hate me."

But I do. I hate her. In this moment, there is nothing I feel more than hatred for this young woman. What does she mean she can't do this? This, *this*, is all she's planned on since finding out she was pregnant. Having a sibling is the one thing Grayson has always wanted. So, yeah, sitting in this parking lot outside of a hotel in Denton, Texas, getting ready to head to the hospital to meet my newborn son, I hate her. When I have to tell Grayson he isn't going to be a big brother, I hate her even more.

This isn't the first time I've lost a baby. It's the third. But this is the first one I lost mere minutes before seeing his face and cradling him in my arms. At least I got to hold the other two, see them in real life and not just an ultrasound photo. I also had to bury the other two, so maybe this way is better after all.

When I was seventeen, a doctor told me it would be a miracle if I ever got pregnant. Something even experts couldn't quite pinpoint was making a mess of my reproductive system. I had my first period at twelve, and fewer than twenty total by seventeen, which is why doctors were even looking at my childbearing potential while I was still in high school. I didn't plan to have children, so my response to hearing this news was literally a shoulder shrug and an "oh, well" smirk.

In spite of what doctors said, I got pregnant at twenty-seven. The pregnancy was easy, no issues or concerns, and the delivery was perfect. Maybe they'd gotten it wrong all those years ago, or maybe my body had corrected the issues over time. Not that it mattered. I didn't want to have more kids. Moreover, the father of my child vanished six weeks postpartum, and once I became a single parent babies weren't on my mind at all.

Babies *were* on Grayson's mind, though. Constantly. He's naturally gregarious and no amount of company ever fully satisfied him, so living alone with his introverted mother was tantamount to torture. Over and over he asked when he could have a sibling. I wasn't in a position to fill that request, but it broke my heart to see him lonely and longing. Growing up an only child was heaven for me. For him, it was hell, so I tried to find a way to make him a big brother.

One day a colleague shared how a student had approached her years before, asking if she knew anyone who wanted to adopt a baby. The young lady wasn't ready for baby and was terrified to tell her parents she was pregnant. I learned this request was not uncommon at our university. Suddenly, I knew how to get a sibling for Grayson.

I would pray.

I was specific in my prayer because Grayson was specific in his request for a sibling who "matched" him. For years I prayed someone on campus would approach me and ask if I wanted to adopt a biracial baby. No such thing happened.

Slowly I stopped praying for it. Grayson was getting older, and school and friends helped with the loneliness, and he was actually growing more attached to being an only child. Eventually, I forgot about the prayer altogether.

Two years after I stopped praying for a baby, a man showed up. Not just any man—*the* man. Falling in love was not in my plans, but it happened anyway. He was also a single parent, someone who understood my life and was willing to accept my kid. One of the most loving, genuine people I've ever met, he quickly thawed and won my icy heart. But when I found out I was pregnant, mere months into our relationship, I was scared. I hadn't thought about having another child since I stopped praying for an adoption miracle. Did I even want one? Did *he*? I didn't know.

I didn't give him the chance to tell me either, as I withdrew from him and into myself to try to make sense of everything. It took two weeks for me to work though my fear and anxiety. Once I did, I was ready to tell him and see what happened. The day before I planned to go to his house and share, I woke up in pain. It felt as though my insides were shredding. Tears streamed down my face. I desperately needed to go to the bathroom. Once I sat on the toilet, I had a strong urge to push.

No. NO. This couldn't be happening.

Bolts of pain continued to shoot through my abdomen as I tried to urinate and tried not to push. *Splop.* The pain eased as I heard it. I didn't want to look, but I had to. I'd miscarried. A scream escaped me as I saw the red mass in the toilet bowl. I saw the stringy tissue floating from the edges, the clotted places dense and dark as night. I saw the small, translucent sac, and in it a tiny, lima bean-shaped embryo. My baby. Perhaps the doctors had been right after all.

I couldn't leave it there, floating in toilet water and urine. It pained me enough that it had to be in there at all. I slowly reached in and slid my hand beneath the mass, cupping it gently as I lifted it from the water. Even though it further broke my fractured heart, I looked at it closely, taking advantage of the only time I'd ever have with my child. I tenderly wrapped it in a tissue and placed it in a tiny Altoids tin, which I later buried in my flower garden.

When I finally saw him, I told him everything. His face lit up when I said I'd gotten pregnant, only to darken when I told him I'd miscarried. He cried, as much for me having to go through it alone as for our loss. The silver lining, though, was we talked about our future and whether or not we wanted it to include more kids.

We did.

I started taking better care of myself and making sure my body was a strong home for a pregnancy. Six months after miscarrying, I had a positive pregnancy test. Calculations indicated I'd gotten pregnant on Christmas Day, a guaranteed miracle if ever there was one. We were together when I took this test, and we took a couple selfies to commemorate the occasion. His eyes were red from crying happy tears, but the joy still shone brightly. The next morning I took Grayson to see *Kung Fu Panda 2*. When I had to rush out of the theater and into the bathroom, doubled over in pain, I knew there were no miracles for me.

I'm thankful my body was gracious enough not to expel this embryo in the toilet at Alamo Drafthouse. It had the decency to wait until we got home. I thought knowing what was coming would make things easier to deal with. Wrong. From the *splop* to the mass in the toilet to the water rescue to staring at my precious embryo lying in a tissue in my palm, every step felt crueler. This was supposed to be our Christmas miracle baby. Instead, it was conclusive evidence the doctors were right. Grayson had been the miracle baby after all.

As fate would have it, the next December my prayer from years before was answered. While walking across campus, a friend approached me and asked, "Do you want to adopt a baby?" I laughed, thinking she was joking. She wasn't. "There's a girl having a baby soon. The first family fell through. She's looking for an interracial couple—black dad, white mom. The baby is biracial."

Us. She wanted her baby—the baby that matched exactly what I prayed for in every way—to have us.

Within a week we were talking to the birth mother, we had a lawyer, and our community was graciously helping us raise the money needed for adoption fees. My husband and I were excited to finally have a baby together. Grayson was *thrilled* to finally become a big brother. We were getting our miracle after all!

On January 2nd, at 2:46 a.m., a text message woke me: "I'm having contractions. We're going to the hospital."

It was time!

I replied: "We're praying! We'll pack our bags and get on the road!"

The trip that normally takes five hours took almost nine, thanks to slick roads and icy precipitation, but we didn't care. We were on our way to meet our baby! She and I texted throughout the day, and when she couldn't text, her grandmother sent updates about how things were progressing. Grayson and I settled into our hotel and impatiently waited, trash TV and junk food keeping us company. There was no news before bedtime, so we tucked in, though our excitement kept us from sleeping well.

I texted her as soon as I woke up. He was here! She told me how perfect he was, how well he slept, and how sad she was as they took him to be circumcised. I should've seen the signs. Instead of realizing he'd been born the night before and we hadn't been notified, I naively asked her if we could head to the hospital to meet him. "Of course!" she replied. "Can't wait!"

That was a lie.

Grayson and I quickly put on our coats and braved the winter weather to go meet our miracle. We'd just buckled in when *ding*!

No. NOT AGAIN. I cannot lose another baby.

"God wants me to keep my baby. Please don't hate me."

Apparently, I can.

I didn't even have the words to reply. I was too blinded by rage. Then there was a second *ding*! This one from her grandmother: "It was such a hard decision for her. She's so worried she's hurt your feelings." Hurt my feelings? The absurdity would've made me laugh had I not been so angry.

Telling Grayson was every bit as awful as I feared. He drew his knees to his chest, becoming a tight little ball in the passenger seat, and stared. One shaky word escaped before the tears took over. "Why?" I didn't have an answer.

We were scheduled to stay in the area for three days, long enough to pass the mandatory waiting period for adoptions in Texas and take our baby boy home with us, but I no longer saw the point. The drive home was silent, sorrow and anger filling every space. Once home I was grateful to find my husband had removed every trace of adoption preparation. Grayson went directly to his room to be alone. I fell into bed and cried.

I've never felt such deep pain and despair as I did over the next few days. As I cried through the night, my body physically hurt in ways and places I'd never felt before. I couldn't imagine how I would ever recover. Not a third time.

But I did. Thanks to my family and friends who held me up, my heart healed completely. I can see babies and baby things and not weep or become angry. I can think about the babies who didn't become part of our family and not despair. On that cold day in January, I couldn't believe life would ever be good again. But it is, and I am thankful.

Bio: *Shenai Moore is passionate about social justice, true equality, and empowering marginalized voices. She is also passionate, though less so, about books, cats, college football, and Tupac Shakur. An assistant professor of English, Shenai is an Enneagram 5 with a 6 wing. She doesn't really know what that means, but finding out brought her students much joy. As clichéd as it may sound, her husband, Kevin, is her best friend and her son, Grayson, is her heart.*

CRONESHADOW
STUMBLES AHEAD

by Polly Atkin

The Invisible

Croneshadow stumbles ahead of me   catching
erratic feet on the tarmac   ruched
as it is by roots   her left foot sticking
as if in mud   her stoop cranked up
by the pockmarked skin of the drystone wall
she is thrown on   the angle of light   sickish
orange in the early night.   Her mouth
twitches down at the creases   *Bitchy
Resting Face*   though you cannot see it
dark on dark.   You could say she exists
in relief   except there is none   not
for a structure like her   misbuilt   collapsing
inward with each jolt forward. I try
to right her but she will not straighten. The more

I struggle the more she looks broken. She knows
more of pain than your charts can trace
but you will not acknowledge her   hear her. Her name
is a slur. Her body is carrion. It is
too late for this.

                    My blood too sticky.
Her edges are blurring.

                        My legs are unraveling.
Her gown of bones is clacking   clacking.
Will we ever reach home?

                        I sink in my clothes
'til my breath melts the frost on the empty road.
She pushes ahead of me   carries on walking.
Carries on walking.

                    Carries on walking.

*

I wrote "The Invisible" on a winter night in 2014 or
early 2015, not long after I was diagnosed with hyper-
mobile Ehlers Danlos syndrome, a hereditary connect-
ive tissue disorder characterized by joint hypermobility
and tissue fragility. It is caused by a difference in the
structure of collagen, the structure that keeps us to-
gether, that forms our tendons, ligaments, bone, muscle,
cartilage, and skin. I cannot keep myself together. I am
in a continual process of falling apart, of falling away
from myself, of falling away myself in time.

*

crone (n.)

late 14 c., "a feeble and withered old woman," in Middle English a strong term of abuse, from Anglo-French *carogne* "carrion, carcass; an old ewe," also a term of abuse, from Old North French *carogne*, Old French *charogne*, term of abuse for a cantankerous or withered woman, also "old sheep," literally "carrion," from Vulgar Latin **caronia*. Literally Carrion.

*

In her essay "Peering into the dark of the self, with selfie," Sonya Huber writes about taking "pain selfies." She writes:

"My pain selfies mark time, though I haven't collected them consciously [...] I surface from pain and want to see myself. Or I want to record that I have reached a mile marker on an invisible trail."

She takes them, perhaps, to record change, transformation through pain, "to understand the full scope of what [she] lives with."

The pain selfie becomes a "private signpost to remember that what I feel is real."

The pain selfie is a record of the other woman she is in pain, who she calls Pain Woman,

both herself and not herself. Pain Woman
knows things Sonya Huber does not.

She is the creature I have called Croneshadow
in this poem, a "woman linked by blood but
whom I barely know."

Huber calls her "that woman, myself."

*

As soon as I began to take photographs I
began to take photographs of my self—my
self as my shadow, as my reflection, half
caught in windows or mirrors. I preferred my
self in shadow, in fragment. Only half seen.
I couldn't look at my self straight on. I didn't
want to look at my self straight on. My ugli-
ness. My awkwardness. I couldn't even look
my self in the eye.

I liked my self better in shadow.

I liked my self better stretched out, drawn out.
Bunched up. I knew my self better that way.

I liked my self better when my distortion is
visible.

I know my self better when my distortion is
visible.

*

shadow (n.)

Old English *sceadwe*, *sceaduwe* "the effect of interception of sunlight, dark image cast by someone or something when interposed between an object and a source of light," oblique cases ("to the," "from the," "of the," "in the") of *sceadu* (see shade **(n.)**). *Shadow* is to *shade* (n.) as meadow is to *mead* (n.2). Similar formation in Old Saxon *skado*, Middle Dutch *schaeduwe*, Dutch *schaduw*, Old High German *scato*, German *schatten*, Gothic *skadus* "shadow, shade."

From mid-13 c. as "darkened area created by shadows, shade." From early 13 c. in sense "anything unreal"; mid-14 c. as "a ghost"; late 14 c. as "a foreshadowing, prefiguration." Meaning "imitation, copy" from 1690s. Sense of "the faintest trace" from 1580s; that of "a spy who follows" from 1859.

*

Sometimes the lens of the camera can translate matter into image that the lens of the human eye cannot decipher. Aurora borealis, blur motion, sun damage, distant stars, spirit. Very small detail, very wide view.

Is it taking it too far to expect the camera can capture her, that woman, myself, Croneshadow? That the camera can turn my invisible pain into visual signals? That it can fix her in a moment in time, like the spectral being she is? The spy that follows. That pinned in the frame of the photograph, she becomes evidence? That I can keep her there, like a pet. That I can exhibit her there, proof of life. That a photograph is enough to justify belief? That if I get it right, the right angle, the right light, I will be believed.

*

"The Invisible" is both a shadow portrait and a pain selfie. It is a love poem to her, Croneshadow, that other me who keeps going when I can't. It is a record of her existence. It insists on the reality of her experience. It insists on her presence.

*

I don't like the phrase "invisible disabilities"; "invisible illness." It has felt that way, for sure, but can I afford to wait for someone to see me? Whole lifetimes pass like this, in pain, in distress, unseen, unheard. Medical ghosts flitting through the hospital corridors. Even the experts—those who have pored over images of us in textbooks—

cannot see us. Refuse to see us. We disturb their rooms, ruffle their papers with our cold breath, hover over them as they sleep in their chairs screaming *acknowledge me acknowledge me*. But we are invisible. We are ghosts. We are fictional. We are stranger things and we do not exist to them.

You cannot see what you refuse to admit is real.

Ghosts do not exist. People are not shadows.

To call us invisible is to erase us, to keep erasing us, to rub us out cell after cell day after day. We walk into a room as solid and human as anyone, but the word *invisible* renders us immaterial. To call us invisible is to give the power to the perceiver and the perceiver's perception.

Some prefer *hidden* or *unseen*.

Disability Studies gives us *non-apparent*.

The motto of the Ehlers Danlos Society is "making our invisible, visible." But we are not invisible. We are unseen. Unrecognized. Actively ignored.

I see your pain because I know what it looks like, I know that downturn of my own mouth, that vacant frown.

It is not invisible. You are not invisible. I see you. I see you as I see myself.

*

If a person is a shadow they can only be seen when the light is shining on them. They need to be brought to light. They need original response. They need to be acknowledged by the light as a solid form, as real. The light makes the invisible visible.

Do you think that when there is no light our shadows are with us, like the moon in the day, outside the visible spectrum, ghost shadows, spirit shadows?

*

The self as foot. The self as eye. The self as footprint in sand, in snow. The self as half a face. Turned away, or turning. The self as shadow.

*

In her book, *Invisible*, a book that explores how women live with invisible conditions, how they manage the problem of invisibility, Michelle Lent Hirsch writes about how sickness manifests as "deathyness." The spectre of mortality. Even when disability is hidden to the abled gaze, its meaning, its shadow, Pain Woman, the crone, shines through the skin as *deathyness*. The whiff of rot.

162

*

There are photos I can't look at because they remind me of my pain. They might seem entirely ordinary to anyone else. But I can read the sickness in my eyes, their shadows, their glossy surface, their half-hooded gaze. My forced and unconvincing smile. The unsavory tone of my skin. I don't want to look at it. I see my own deathyness and it sickens me. I see how others cannot see it, and that is worse.

*

The crone is not about age. The crone is always there. The crone has always been there.

She is the carrion in me. The parts of me others see as dead meat. I am dead meat, and she is me.

I have been dead meat all my life.

*

Croneshadow knows things I don't know. When I say she is carrion, it is a double pun. She is a slur in the mouths of the ignorant, those who see her as a carcass, as rotten, as food for crows, but when the crows eat her she flies with them. She sees with their eyes and has their abilities. She sees everything from inside and also from above, in flight. She continues. She carries on.

She knew before I did that my blood was too sticky and that its stickiness was dangerous, pathological: a symptom of genetic hemochromatosis, iron toxicity swelling my red blood cells, before I had heard of it, a year before I would learn of it.

She has access to the arcane. She is the part of myself that reaches beyond this plane. She brings messages and knowledge from the other side. From the past of my body and beyond it, far into the deep past of my genetic code. From the future I cannot yet imagine, the selves I will be, and will shed.

She knows how to sustain. She knows when to lie down in the road and cry. She knows when to eat and when to be eaten. She is a continual process of re-becoming. She is nothing and everything. She is the closest thing to holy I know, and everything I am is because of her.

Do you see her?

Now?

Now?

Now?

Bio: *Polly Atkin lives in Cumbria. Her first full poetry collection Basic Nest Architecture (Seren: 2017) is followed by a third pamphlet, With Invisible Rain (New Walk Press: 2018). Her first pamphlet bone song (Aussteiger, 2008) was shortlisted for the Michael Marks Pamphlet Award, 2009, and second, Shadow Dispatches (Seren, 2013), won the Mslexia Pamphlet Prize, 2012. She is working on a hybrid memoir exploring place, chronic illness and belonging. In 2019 she co-founded the Open Mountain initiative with Kendal Mountain Festival, which seeks to center voices that are currently at the margins of outdoor, mountain and nature writing.*

POETRY

FIGHTING WITH WATER

by Eden Julia Sugay

Our blood is poison for the body it fills is female.
Our names are not ours and we are unclaimed
unwanted and fighting with water from birth.

We were graced with three protectors
possessing fierce instincts to battle the sea
and keep the water from forcing more cracks in us.

We are ashamed of the protection we need
wanting for nothing more than to fight back on
   behalf of our defenders;
without power, what is our place here?

Everyone says three is a crowd,
surely five is heavy enough to make you drown.
Year after year we start to believe *maybe we do belong*
   barred to that blue salted floor.

My sister, we are the dusty excess of our ancestors
stealing time from the night to laugh aloud in the
    face of our dark oceans.
Laughing to bide our time until we can recover
    the rights stripped of us

        until we are enough

Bio: *Eden Julia Sugay received her B.A. in Creat-
ive Writing from Mills College and is a Poetry Editor
for Apricity Press.*

*Her writing highlights her voice as a queer woman of
color and reflects on navigating identity and relationships,
and their constantly evolving natures. Eden is inspired by
the sun and the pink-faced, glossy-eyed details of honesty
(read: she is a Cancer sun-Cancer rising-Aries moon, and
a huge advocate of crying). Her work has appeared in
The Walrus and Kissing Dynamite.*

*When Eden isn't frantically jotting half-formed
thoughts on the edges of napkins or on her phone's notes,
she likes to fill her time dancing, baking, and exploring
new ways love can manifest.*

FOR WOMEN IN(ARE) OCEANS

by Elle Arra

there's a homeless woman lying in leisure pain
on an eighteen hundred thread count island
somewhere in the devil's triangle. she moved
to the Atlantic Ocean hoping to find the lost
treasures that had been taken from her
abandoned body.

it's not just things like planes and ships that go missing here

whole women go missing, hopes, promise, flesh.
the breasts go, but those can be reconstructed or
held up with fabric and wire. the bones go, but there
are supplements for that. unspoken memoirs furrow
the brow, the face pleats and puckers, but there are
creams and exercises for that. the soul stops
  singing—

there is no treatment for this

no artificial remedy. you must take the stones from your pockets, resurface from your ocean bed, you must expel the water from your lungs and pull the shore to your mouth. woman, you are a high tide. did no one tell you that you are the ocean? you can swallow islands whole.

Bio: *Elle Arra, a Michigan native, is a visual artist, poet, and writer currently working and residing in the sultry foothills of the Appalachian Mountains in Madison, AL. Graduating Magna Cum Laude from the HBCU Oakwood University as a "late bloomer – over the age of 40" is some- thing she takes great pride in and has inspired her to cre- ate a forthcoming scholarship for other women over the age of 40 endeavoring to complete higher education. Her work has been published in print and online publications such as Hypertrophic Literary, Figroot Press, Corvus Review, The Valley Planet, and more. She also wrote the foreword "Native and Alien"; for the book "Some Days, Here"; a collection of poems by Tricia De Jesus-Gutierrez. On a given day you can find her tending peonies, freestyling or flowing (mostly 90s golden era hip-hop), watching live theatre, or decorating something– reminding us that style and beauty matter.*

WILLOW ON ALLT NAN CLACH SGOILTE

by Leonie Charlton

I felt the tree before I found it.

Felt it when I was lying down in the Shepherd's Bothy near to where the burn of the split stones meets the River Kinglass. Felt something growing my body to water-plaited grace. A purr of song and stretch, spinal twist, limbs longing toward their potential. Of course it was sexual.

All this beneath the rakery of a hooded crow on a tarred tin roof.

When I found the tree Annie Lennox's "Here Comes the Rain Again" was rilling through my head. The lyrics surprised me in the sunshine. As did the willow, the way it took me by the scruff and shook me loose, the way I understood things: like how when you've stood so many storms your flowers blow sooner; how one being can have this many beginnings; how bared roots untangle a day, a life; how much is said between sage tongues; how circles of resistance grow under lichen. Mostly I understood that this tree was a dream coming right at me from the boulderous banks.

Bio: *Leonie Charlton lives on the west coast of Scotland. She writes creative non-fiction, poetry and fiction. Her work has appeared in publications such as Causeway, Northwords Now, and The Blue Nib. Her first full-length book, Marram, was published by Sandstone Press in March 2020. Marram is the story of her journey through the Outer Hebrides with Highland ponies; the travelogue is intercut with intimate memoir as she leaves behind beads in memory of her mother. Leonie won the Cinnamon Press Poetry Pamphlet Prize in 2020 and her pamphlet 'Ten Minutes of Weather Away' will be published in early 2021. Much of her writing is based on a sense of place and our relationship with other species and the natural world. Learn more at www.leoniecharlton.co.uk.*

1999

by Katie Hale

In the communal changing rooms where old
   women's bodies
flapped and scattered droplets like pieces of
   crystal,
we contorted ourselves behind the bright flags of
   towels, wished
together for the other pool—the one with lockers
   and locked doors,

where the air was jungle thick and cubicles close
   with damp—
where once I saw your chest raised like a ripple
   of water.
You whispered *look*, showed me the first kindling
   of hair,
and I had to ask *does it hurt?* so you said *feel it—see?*
   soft—like a bird—

Though you meant only one bird, the sparrow
   in the old byre,
battering itself bloody against the glass, 'til your
   dad
caught it, said *girls*, said *don't be afraid*, and kept it
quaking between his hands for us to stroke.

In the pool, my stomach is too bare, and a man
with ribs like a shelf of dusty Reader's Digests
   watches me swim.

Bio: *Born in Cumbria, Katie Hale is the author of a novel,* My Name is Monster *(Canongate, 2019) and two poetry pamphlets:* Breaking the Surface *(flipped eye, 2017) and* Assembly Instructions *(Southword, 2019), which won the Munster Chapbook Prize. She is a former MacDowell Fellow, and has held a number of international Writer in Residence positions. She regularly runs writing workshops for adults and in schools, and is currently working on a first full-length poetry collection, funded by Arts Council England.*

WILDLING

by Jay Caldwell

Whooping I whirl through the air.
Ducks and dragonflies dart to safety
as my shadow eclipses the brook.
I'm off up The Billing with my mates.

Today I'm still one of the boys.
Freckled and flat-chested I could pass for one,
hand-me-down shorts flap round sparrow legs,
my knees scarred with happy memories.

The day feels timeless.
Pre-mobile phones, our ears are tuned
to the ring of our mothers shouting us in for tea
from the fields behind the factory.

Legs whipped to wheals by summer grasses
we trudge home—
just enough energy to trip each other up,
squeezing the last from the darkening day.

With a final thump on the arm
and a "see ya tomorrow, yeah?"
I head indoors to Findus crispy pancakes
and the threat of a bath.

Tomorrow when I call round
Paul and Tim will scuff their shoes
on the orange lino at their back door
and say they can't come out.

That afternoon I'll spot them at the Tarn.
They'll jut their chins as I run to join them,
and I'll be shocked to learn that overnight
this wildling has become just a girl.

Bio: *Jay Caldwell is a poet who lives and writes at the edge of Peak District. Many of her poems gain inspiration from the hills surrounding her home. Living with many health conditions, and disabled by society, she spends her non-writing times advocating for those whose voice is still not heard. She lives with her husband, and rescue dog. Her poems have appeared in a variety of publications and anthologies including Faith, Hope and Fiction and the Thomas Merton Journal.*

GOALIE GLOVES

by Jane Patience

Standing, cold between the posts.
Eleven years of tiny muscle, unfused bone.
Daring them to do their worst,
you brace now as they take their kicks, you stand
  alone.

Skinny arms made Minnie Mouse
by giant goalie gloves, your ticket to respect,
though they start to notice now
and so do you, the narrowing waist and budding
  breast.

So, made self-conscious by your
slender length of neck and gentle clavicle slope,
you will scarf up and pad out,
but cannot hide the pout, the upturned Cupid's bow,
a subtle grace with every throw,
the azure flash from underneath each lengthy lash.

Resilient, hard and tough.
You're one of them for now but, Sweet, I'll tell you
    this.
Your boyish days are numbered
and it won't be long before you know what strength *is*.

The girl's team beckons to you
and yes, for now it makes you scoff.
Womanhood approaches fast.
That's when the gloves come off.

Bio: *Jane Patience lives in East Dunbartonshire, Scotland. She completed an MLitt in Creative Writing at Glasgow University in 2008 and has 'dabbled' with writing ever since, having had various short stories and poems published and broadcast on radio. Now in her sixtieth year, she finally has the time to take her writing more seriously.*

ISSUES

by Joanne Bell

I have an issue with the word issue
describing mental health
conditions.

It makes me think of
the way kids talk: *she's* got issues
or when my mum says
"your Dad has an issue with BT."

It's troublesome
bothersome
an insect flicked
from your shoulder
blinking light
on the dashboard
of your car.

According to the dictionary
issues are "personal problems"

like periods
which we learn to manage at thirteen
by hiding them.

Issues are not:
debilitating illnesses
chronic pain
the vacant
hopeless
feeling
that leads to
a conversation
where I say, months into recovery,
I can't guarantee I won't take my own life.

This language is shaming.

It makes me feel
I am the creator
of my illness
and have to be the healer.

When I got sick,
I say now.

When I was really ill.

People tend not to ask any more.

Bio: *Joanne Bell is an Edinburgh-based writer and poet with credits in literary magazines including Northwords Now Salomé and Luminous, Defiant, an anthology by Listen Softly Press. Performances include The Bowery Poetry Club in New York, 'That's What She Said' at the Edinburgh Fringe and many other events. Her prose was selected for the Edinburgh International Book Festival's emerging writer program and her debut novel longlisted for the Agora Books Work in Progress Prize 2019. She also runs Write to Thrive, therapeutic writing designed to help women connect, reflect, and empower themselves. www. joannebell.org*

SECRET ME

by Leela Soma

Cradled in the tropics, a nascent soul
cherished, nourished, a protected bud
blossomed then uprooted to an alien land
laden with a secret, the heritage of privilege
buried deep inside, as voices bandied words
of hurt, Paki, slum-dog, poverty. Muted
I accepted and blended. The new marginalized me
the scars deep, keloid hard, an interred Brahmin,
forever shedding the skin of my rich culture.

Bio: *Leela Soma was born in Madras, India and now lives in Glasgow, Scotland, UK. Her poems and short stories have been published in a number of anthologies, publications. She has published two novels and two collections of poetry. She has served on the Scottish Writer's Centre Committee and is now on East Dunbartonshire Arts & Culture Committee and The Sottish Pen Women Writers Committee. Some of her work reflects her dual heritage of India and Scotland. She was nominated for the Pushcart Prize 2020.*

WHERE I AM FROM/ HALF THE STORY

after George Ella Lyon
by Tanatsei Gambura

I am from Lazarous,
the figment of my father's memory whom I will
    never meet.
I am from his wife's red-roofed house (a familiar,
    lost friend tucked
cozily in the hem of Mbare's old underclothing),
from Mbuya's copper wristbands, her sapphire
headwrap of the holy Anglican Church, her kit-
    chen; her favorite secret,
where chibage was cooked to a sweet, soft pulp.
I am from the township adjacent to hers, the
    crescent shape of
Glenview Area 8. I am from the erupting sound
    of buoyant giggles,
the blaring of a 2002 radio in Mbuya Chihera's
    compound.

I am from the home of Lazarous's mistress, the
   woman who
birthed my father: Gogo, whose home was once
a resting place for travelers.
I am from a woman who rolled folktales from her
   tongue
like a cinema house during a school holiday,
I am from her lightly salted mbambaira:
fat tubers enjoyed at a late, noisy breakfast, the sun
   peaking overhead,
glittering through a shady lemon tree.
I am from her rich Tanganda tea, sweetened with
   thick, creamy milk
and the sweet sugar of her spirit. I am from her rituals:
the grace with which she cooled the steaming brew,
   pouring it
leisurely into a flat metal dish, blowing discipline
   into its harsh heat.
I am also from another place, a distant, lone house
   kwaSeke,
firmly pressed into the fine albino sands of the out-
   skirts.
I am from the curious, gaping tunnel in the ground,
   the well
Gogo Chijota extracted water from,
the round hut that enclosed her hearth, ashy
   residue floating

onto the polished walls, into my black hair.
I am from her adopted son, the boy who
was called Simba, another memory that would
    slip
Chichewa off its tongue when sitting in the house
    of elders.

I am from returning.
I am from returning to the manicured lawn of a
suburban house in pre-election Westgate, to
    bottle brushes,
palms, and open cycads. To the smell of Alsatians
    in my arms.
I am from the private hills of Arcturus,
a place of bounty where the sweet flesh of
    mazhanje in the summer
bursts in my mouth—fresh, warm, welcoming—
rare, like a memory.

Notes

Mbare:	the oldest township in Harare. It is known for squalor and poverty.
Mbuya:	Shona word for grandmother.
Chibage:	Shona word for corn.
Mbambaira:	sweet potatoes.
Gogo:	Shona alternative word for grandmother.
Tanganda:	the largest tea grower in Zimbabwe.
KwaSeke:	the name of a rural area on the outskirts of Harare.
Chichewa:	a Bantu language spoken primarily in Malawi, Zambia and Zimbabwe.
Westgate:	the name of a suburb in Harare. It used to be an affluent suburb before its gradual decline.
Arcturus:	a forested area on the outskirts of Harare
Alsatian:	a breed of dog.
Mazhanje:	wild, indigenous sugar plum fruit, Uapaca kirkman. Summer growing season.

THE CONCEPTION OF TRAGEDY

by Tanatsei Gambura

The condition of whiteness is that of two children:
one who prays fervently in fear of burning in hell,
and the other who identifies with God's male prefix
and the color of his skin.

What is blasphemy if not the child
who cannot wrap their tongue around their own
    name?
These are the things we do not know how to name.
Listen to the languages I have been taught:
    this child of a violent act I keep close behind my
    front teeth—

        a convenience,

                neuyu mutauro unemazwi

> anoshisha asati abuda mukanwa,
> oramba kubuda mukanwa.[1]

We never speak of language as inconvenient, or
    as a disability.
If the truth is a threat, history will be dishonest.
That is to say, our bodies are history,
an archive of the untrue.

There are days when it is too much,
days when I starve myself and sew my lips to-
    gether with wire.
I refuse to open my mouth—my words are a
    river that does not meet

                                        the sea.

Bio: *Tanatsei Gambura is a poet and cultural practitioner
from Zimbabwe. She is the runner-up to the inaugural
Amsterdam Open Book Prize for the manuscript Things
I Have Forgotten Before where the enclosed poems feature.
Drawing from personal experience, her work explores the
themes of black womanhood in the context of post-colonial
immigration, global geopolitics and cultural identity.*

---

1 *neuyu mutauro unemazwi anoshisha asati abuda mukanwa, oramba
kubuda mukanwa:* Shona loosely translates to *and this language
whose words ferment before they escape the mouth, then refuse to leave
the mouth altogether.*

Poems of hers appear in Prufrock Magazine, the London Reader and New Coin Poetry Journal among others. She is an alumnus of the British Council residency, "These Images are Stories" and has been recognised by United Nations Women and the Goethe Institut.

YOU WILL NEVER TAKE MY VOICE

by Linda M. Crate

we were in mixed company,
and i can't remember
who brought the subject up
or why it came up;
but i remember what you said
to this very day—
children of rapists should
all be aborted,
you said,
and whilst i will always fight
for a woman's right to choose
her own path
that cut and dry statement
cut me to the core;
because my father was a monster
who hurt my mother and i will forever be

grateful she chose to give me life—
she told me once that sometimes
beautiful things
come from terrible circumstances,
and i know she was talking about me;
you may not see my magic or my worth
and you may not speak my language or know
the power of my dreams—
but you will never take my voice,
i've got songs to sing.

I'M A GIFT, NOT A CURSE

by Linda M. Crate

you called me "queer girl",
and i will admit that those words
did wound me, at first;
no doubt you thought yourself witty
or you were trying to impress
your friend—

the next day my hands trembled
when i grabbed my rainbow beanie,
i didn't even want to place it
upon my head;

but i told myself i wouldn't let you have
the last laugh and that victory would be mine—

i am a survivor and a warrior,
and i will never surrender myself

to anyone who would destroy
me for any reason;

i've got dreams and goals of my own to
    accomplish—

this queen won't be conquered or slowed down
by those who don't know that being different
is a gift, not a curse.

Bio: *Linda M. Crate is a writer whose works have been published in numerous magazines and anthologies both online and in print. She is the author of six poetry chapbooks, the latest of which is: More Than Bone Music (Clare Songbirds Publishing House, March 2019). She is also the author of the novel Phoenix Tears (Czykmate Books, June 2018). Recently she has published two full-length poetry collections Vampire Daughter (Dark Gatekeeper Gaming, February 2020) and The Sweetest Blood (Cyberwit, February 2020).*

LITTLE GIRL PINK

by Gayle Smith

It was a challenge,
knowing who I was
but not being able say
at nights I would pray to waken up right
but the day never came
fear, guilt, and shame,
the triplets that haunted my teens
I was scared to be myself
except on Halloween
the one day of the year I felt normal
in the ladies formal wear
my mother would select as my outfit
the desperate housewife of Maryhill
was the look my inner girl was given
and accepted without complaint
well better that than a pirate
or other boy-related stuff
it was tough but I did what I had to do

little boy blue was for one night only
little girl pink
it was a difficult road
growing up when I did
but it prepared me for later life
and the barriers I would face
this world can be a cruel place
for those who don't fit in
to the boxes society selects
respect not easily earned
for those who fight the system
I think this is why
many trans women of my generation
left it later than we'd like before transitioning
social and cultural conditioning plays
a part in all our lives
whether we like it or otherwise
to deny this reality
is only to lie to ourselves
and that's something I was taught never to do
and the reason little boy blue
became little girl pink
at an age when she knew her own worth
and how to serve God's purpose
in ways she could never have imagined
before beginning her journey

ACCIDENTAL GIRL

by Gayle Smith

I don't think she would ever admit it
not even to her closest friends
but to me my mother feminized me
and whether she knew it or not
raised an accidental daughter
and molded her in Presbyterian guilt

of course in my childhood years
such a notion would have been dismissed
I was eight in '69
that magical time of Woodstock, men on the
   moon and the stonewall riots
sailed past a quiet child

I had health concerns
my future labeled by experts
who as it turns out didn't know
quite as much as they'd like to think

ACCIDENTAL GIRL

I tended toward pink rather than blue
and loved the shade she painted my nails
on the day Ann Jones won the Wimbledon
    ladies final

I wasn't an only child
an older brother was allowed to discover
the great outdoors
climbing trees and playing football
while I went to the shops
listened to small talk
and knew the difference
between every cut of meat in the butchers
before all the other kids
in the scheme

whether she knew it or not
my mother was shaping my future
in ways she could never have foreseen
when I was 12 or 13 I was allowed to buy Jackie
but woman's own was to be my compulsory
weekly reading

this she said was to remind me
of the drudgery of her daily existence
I was permitted to dress in private
and fitted in panty girdles

to give me a female shape
when pancakes as she called them
didn't have the filling for a bra

she tried to convince herself
it would go away
my escape from the male gender cage just
    happened because I was bored
it annoyed her when she realized
that my female desires and dreams could no
    longer be ignored
she couldn't content herself and say
it was just a rebellious phase
even though she was terrified of
the social plague
or as I called it neighborhood gossip

she knew the truth of my real identity
    though sexuality was never discussed
she realized I had longings and lusts like a
    daughter not a son
though god knows she blushed at the thought
    of them
not that I would say too much to her after all
    she raised me to be ladylike and in that at
    least, her lassie
played by her rules

fast forward to the present day
you can see it was no phase or seven-day
   wonder
thunder didn't strike me down
nor did the sky fall in
on the accidental girl
who became more like her mother
than she'd ever like to admit

Bio: *Gayle Smith is a trans woman and spoken word poet who co-hosts the long-running Words and Music Open Mic Night with her close friend Jen Hughes at Milk Café on the south side of Glasgow. She has performed at venues across Scotland since 1993. Gayle is a member of Women With Fierce Words and the Scotland Women's National Team Poetry Society. She is also a regular performer with Other Voices Cabaret at the Edinburgh Fringe, and has appeared at Glasgow's leading LGBT cabaret night, Allsorts Cabaret. Her writing has been featured in Mind the Time, Best of 10Red, Women With Fierce Words, Poetry in the Time of Coronavirus, and Hampden Collection.*

THE WHOLE PALAVER (EDITED VERSION)

by Fiona Ritchie Walker

I want you to be waiting at home so I can stomp
   down the hall,
tell you how many times I had to correct her
   spelling,
that she couldn't find *Minister of Religion* on the drop
down screen, typed it in by hand, muttering *R-E-L*
you'll have to help me with this one
then asked my occupation.
When I said *writer* she lifted her head
Are you sure?
Wouldn't something else be more fitting?

My role of carer was three days in the past,
so I stuck with my first choice, then she got
to my employer, said with a smile
a publisher perhaps? I was fizzing.

THE WHOLE PALAVER (EDITED VERSION)

She faffed on, trying to find freelance, self-em-
    ployed,
lost the cursor, added an extra *p* to my name,
though I'd spelled it out before.

When she asked my relationship and I said *wife,*
she told me *not any more,* entered *widow* in the box,
printed out a sheet for me to check, I proofread
twice, just to be sure, then signed with her slanted
    nib
that's at the wrong angle for left handers like me
and in my pause she piped up,
unless you use that fountain pen, it's not legal.

I paid by card, left, was so busy stuffing your
    death
certificates in my bag I almost missed the tur-
    quoise
Sharpie lying on the path, automatically tested
the ink on my hand, sweet gift of a line, my note-
    book open,
sitting on the ground writing out
this whole palaver ending with her name,
then in my head, your generous voice
record, don't shame.

Bio: *Fiona Ritchie Walker was born in Scotland and now lives in England. Her work has been widely published in anthologies and magazines. In 2015 she won the Carer's UK Creative Writing Competition, written after her husband was diagnosed with a terminal lung condition and she became his full-time carer.*

ANECDOTAL SCIENCE

by Claire McFall

Laugh, he told me. Laugh. It's anecdotal
Science. A study in hope. I stared at him, wondering
If he knew what laughter was. If he understood
That the very essence of it was its spontaneity,
An eruption that spews out joy, delight. Gaiety.
A snort, a chuckle, a guffaw. The low tinkle or loud
Rib tickler that warms the air and the eyes.
Did he not realize that laughter had no place in
That cold room, where I spread my legs and my soul,
Hoping he could inject an embryo dream?
Or in the car ride home, where I squeezed my
   thighs together,
Praying I could hold that fragile phantasy inside me?
I said nothing. I went home. I sat in a silent room
And laughed and laughed and laughed.

Three weeks later, my hopes and dreams
Slipped free a red drop at a time.
They died, along with my laughter.

BY THE SEA

by Claire McFall

It's a lovely place to die,
by the sea. If I had to choose a place to let you go,
I can think of no better place than there.
I don't choose, but you go anyway. You leave me
with a whisper, a line on a narrow strip that's a shade
paler than it was the day before. I ponder that strip
all day, again and again, hold it up to the light be-
    side its sister
and try to convince myself that it's a blip, a trick
    of dye
and shadows. It's not. The next day you wave
    goodbye with a
smudge of pink on the tissue. Now I know. Now
    there's no hoping,
no praying, no trying to convince myself of a lie
that's so much easier than the truth.
Out the bathroom window I can see the water,

Uninterrupted by boats, seaside cottages, or
    children playing on the beach.
Just me and the vastness. So long as I stay here, I
    can pretend
that I'm alone with my grief. I don't have to share it
with the voices murmuring downstairs. I am alone;
one soul within this skin once more.

Bio: *Claire McFall is a Scottish writer and former English
teacher now living in sunny Colorado. Her first book, FER-
RYMAN won the 2013 Scottish Children's Book Awards.
TRESPASSERS (2017) and OUTCASTS (2019) com-
plete the series. Her second novel, BOMBMAKER, was
released by Templar Publishing in February 2014 and deals
with terrorism and survival. BLACK CAIRN POINT, re-
leased in the UK by Hot Key Books, won the inaugural Scot-
tish Teenage Book Prize and is a paranormal thriller. Claire
has been published in more than fifteen languages and her
novels have sold more than three million copies worldwide.*

VERTIGO

by Laura Morgan

Botanic Avenue
We push the pram past the station,
Rain drips off my hood.
A rucksack of cash for the builder.
Never has this bag felt so weighted.

The station, the money, my passport
The thought arrows into one;
I could run.

Inca temples
Rainforest lizards
Shorts, mosquito bites
Carnivale: sweat body beets
Euphoria of feet.
Hostel rooftops chats,
Notebook on knees on bumpy buses.
Fruit misshapen, thick skin,

VERTIGO

Seeds and juice dripping down my chin,
Walking in high air, chewing coca leaves
Salt plains bouncing light around my ears
Mountain roads that send my stomach to my toes
Balconies, shutters, dusty brown porches
Hair wrapped in twists of cloths
Itchy jumpers in thick monochromes.

Vertigo unsteadies my feet.

And then the internals:
Burst ventricle
The chambers torn on impact of the train doors.
Every dipple, flashes of youse,
Digs chunks out of my intestine.
No heart left: empty chest cave hemorrhaging,
Leaking blood on strangers,
My loss dragging behind me like prison chains.
Each view layered with the eyes not there.

Three blinks and we are past the station.
Pushing the pram down the hill,
The babes squawking for babychinos.

Bio: *Laura Morgan is a writer and teacher, living in Belfast. She was selected to perform at the Spoken word platform as part of Cúirt International Festival of*

Literature 2019. Her poetry has been published with the Bangor Literary Journal, Abridged Online, and was commended in the Poetry Day HeadStuff competition, 2018. Her first novel 'Stars Apart' is available on Amazon Kindle.

MAMA APPLESKINS

by Kerriann Speers

And I will peel the skin in one smooth caress
Of my knife. Sloughing off the green along with
   the red,
In one long layer slithering onto my plate.
And I will gift them the apple
And they will gum at the glistening white flesh
As they once gorged themselves at my breast.
Juices tripping off their chins.
I will offer up to them
The freshest fruits, the ripest berries, the choicest cuts
And when they do not deign to eat them.
I will peck at their crumbs, like a crow on carrion.
I will go without
Milk for my coffee, so their bones grow long.
Egg for my lunch, so their muscles are strong.
Fish for my plate, so their brains ripen.
I will go without.
I will give them my last
Potato, square of chocolate, segment of orange,

Glass of water, slice of bread, gasp.
If they ask for it.
I will live on appleskins and cold toast crusts.
And I will tell them
Do not run too fast, climb too high, read too late
And I will tell them
Chew your food, clean your teeth, wash your face
And they will say
"I love Daddy more than you, Mama Appleskins"
And "I hate you, Mama Appleskins"
And I will wrap them in blankets
To read them stories from my head.
And I will be Snow Queen and Evil Stepmother,
And Witch disguised as Beggar Woman,
And tricksy fox offering safe passage
And I will eat them up, like gingerbread children.
Snap! Snap! Snap!
And they will laugh and giggle, collapsing on the bed
And sleepily say "Goodnight, Mama Appleskins"
And they will gift me kisses
As sweet as any apple.

Bio: *Kerriann Speers is a fiction writer and poet, published in Writing Magazine and Bangor Literary Journal. A member of Flowerfield Writers Group, Portstewart and Women Aloud NI, Kerriann lives along the North Coast of Ireland. An early school report read "Kerriann reads words that aren't necessarily on the page". This remains true.*

TALL

by Amari Pollard

After years
of
shrinking
myself, of
bending
my limbs
to make
room for
buoyant
bodies and
noisy
mouths,
I'm
struggling
to
remember
how big I
once was.

Bio: *Amari Dawn Pollard is a writer and audience development strategist. She is currently a Park Fellow at the UNC Hussman School of Journalism and Media and previously worked as the Head of Audience Development at The Week. Her creative works have been published in Le Moyne College's annual anthology, The Salamander, and have won her three Newhouse Writing Awards. Amari has also published feature stories at The Week, MindBodyGreen, Bustle, Reader's Digest, and more.*

SHE: A FORCE WHO CAN STOP THE WORLD.

by Fariha Khayyam

O' She,

She who is the light, passed onto the lives of others,
 Brightened with the sacrifices made; willingly.

She who is the flame, lighted generations ago,
 Strengthened with the weight of all the dreams;
 forgotten.

She who is the power, encased and slumbering,
 Resilient with the years of duties; enforced.

Then,
 Why did the world cast her into a shadow?

 They knew she would have become unstoppable.

But now,
  She knows that too.

Bio: *While growing up reading about dragons, magic and adventures, Fariha Khayyam had always wanted to write a book. As her love for reading grew, so did her dream. She began nurturing her dream while completing her Master of Business Administration from Loyola University Chicago, Illinois. Based in Riyadh, Saudi Arabia, when she is not writing, she is found reading fantasy novels or spending time on her social media. You can find her on farihakhayyam.com or on Twitter @fushiee_*

ONE TONGUE

by Imogen. L. Smiley

This tongue in my jaws isn't mine.
It feels foreign against my crooked teeth
I am afraid of it wriggling and writhing
Along the gumline; fighting enamel for a chance
To speak.
I must grind my teeth to hold this tongue.

I have pierced this alien with a bar of silver.
It should keep the monster at bay.
But still, the creature between crimson lips
Paces the cavities of my mouth for an opening.
It rolls my piercing like a joystick; breaking free
Speaking when the rooms are loud.

Little girls aren't allowed to talk about politics.
Little girls aren't allowed to talk about climate change.
Little girls aren't allowed to kiss other little girls.
But little white girls, like me, can protest, without fear
    of harm.

Unlike our sisters of blood, of heart, of identity.
Little girls will scrape knees on tarmac and keep
  going.

Man fears the wrath of these little girls.
The ones who have painted trees along bare legs and
  protested
In jelly sandals instead of going to school.
Man fears the hands of little girls
Who can whittle prosthetic tongues from lint;
And spread the words of feminism.

Man acts in fear against little girls
Acts as a sloppy clothier; crochets lips closed,
Fastens the corners of their mouths into smiles
Man fears men, women, the nonbinary and so,
He confiscates his scissors from those who want to
Change their patterns.

So I have formed an alliance with this tongue.
And I will shout, silver bar and all;
The tongue between my jaws isn't mine.
It's more than just mine—it belongs to everyone,
Whose legs have been sewn shut,
Whose crotches have been "embroidered" with
  F. G. M.

Who have had their tongues severed, by men who
  think they should wield that blade.

This tongue is not mine;
It's theirs
It's ours.

Bio: *Imogen. L. Smiley (she/her), is a twenty-two year old writer from Essex, UK and is a recent Creative & Professional Writing graduate from The University of Derby. She has anxiety, depression and a relentless love of dogs both big and small. Her area of creative focus is primarily gothic literature, but she has been writing poetry since 2016.*

KICKSTARTER BACKERS

I'd like to thank each and every one of our Kickstarter backers, both listed and anonymous, for their contribution to this project. Without you, the creation of *We Are Not Shadows* wouldn't have been possible.

A. K. Tosh
Ali Croal
Alina Corpus
Alice Piotrowska
Alison Liedkie
Allia
Amanda Maneck Spellmire
Amy Pippin Mire
Amy Rose
Andrea Villalobos
Andrew Friedman
Andy Wilkinson
Ange Harker
Angela and Paul Docherty

Angus Morrison
Ann Busby
Annabel Campbell
Anne Rose Cendak
April Langehennig
Arec Rain
Ashleigh H.
Ashley M. Orndorff
Barbara Chaplin
Barbara Gedelian
Becka White
Benjamin Rozzi
Bill Amatneek
Bob and Brenda Fields
Brooke Casper
Brooke Wiles
Bron Hennebry
Buddy H.
C. Lindsay
C. and A. Owen
Calley Carter
Callum Croal
Camille Knepper
Carinn Seabolt
Carole Carroll
Caroline Robinson
Carrye Syma

Catherine Ogston

Celene Barnes

Celine MacLeod

Chellsey Merika Tencati

Chelsea Masquelier

Christie Megill

Christy Rogers, Ph.D.

Claire and Mike McMillan

Claire Squires

Claire Thomson

Claire Withers

Codie Bullen

Corinna Norrick-Rühl

Curtis Spivey

Daniel Chan

Dana Stoddart

Danie K.

Daniel Ballinger

Dante Cross

David McDonald

David Speers

De An Tate

Deb Frost

Deb Todd

Debbie Clark

Denise Lott Arellano

Diana

Eden's Kuya Ian
Elaine Morrison
Electra Rhodes
Elijah Sugay
Elizabeth Wainwright
Elle Arra
Elsa R.
Emma Jones-Gill
Emma Price
Emmie Harrison-West
Ethel Dhlamini-Maqeda
Eve Brodsly
Fion J. Lau
Fiona Ritchie Walker
Firdaus Parvez
Floraidh clement
Gail Spivey
Gavin
Gillian Tasker
Gina Fowler
Hana Said khalfan Al Buraiki
Hannah Poore
Hannah Short
Hannah Ward
Hannah Westwater
Imogen Burns
Isabella J. Mansfield

Izzie Anderson

Jacqueline

Jake Lloyd

James W. Johnson

Jeanne Fury

Jeda Pearl Lewis

Jennifer Dudley

Jennifer Horn

Jen Hughes

Jennyfer Miranda

Jeremy Nelson

Jerry Serrano

Jessica Johnson

Jo Niederhoff

John Phillips

Jonathan Beck

Jonathan Campbell

Jonathan Martin

Jonathan Thomas

Joni Ward

Jordan

Jude Gates

Julia

Julia Patrick

Justin

Kaitlin López

Kaitlyn Hale

Karis Maree

Karla J. Strand

Karlita Gesler

Katalina Watt

Katelynn Young

Katie Over

Katharine D. Owens

Katy Beehler

Kellina Wilkinson

Kelly Peterson

Kerryann Cope

Kevin Castro

K. M.

Kirsten Rees

Kristen Susienka

Krystle Trout

Kyle, Ilyssa, and Darwin

Laura Dodds

Laura Rattray

Leslie Puente

Linda Leek

Lindsey and Mike

Lindsay Middleton

Lindsey B. Nesbitt

Liz and Tyrone Dunbar

Lluvia Estrella

Lois Mead

Lorna Collie

Lorraine Hyslop

Louise Austin

Luke

Lynda Speers

Madeline Bossi

Madelyn Jackson

Maegan Hutton

Mara Driscoll

Marco Buscaglia

Margot Atwell

Maria Medeiros

Marian Waldman

Mark Montellana

Marva Grossman

Maven

Meghan Bradford

Mia BloomBecker

Michael Grimm

Michael J. Hollows

Michaela Whatnall

Michelle Vu

Mimmi Rönning

Monica Plata

Morgan Winder

Morven Gow

Nadia Cureton

WE ARE NOT SHADOWS

Nali McCartney Adesso
Nathan Anderson
Nicole Beaudoin
Nita Soma
Nitya Tripuraneni
Paige Groeneweg
Paul Chada
Paul Alexander Wilson Esq.
Phil Maron
Platon
Polis Loizou
Poppy and Bonnie Speers
Rachel Fowler
Rakie Bennett
Ral Petrova
Rebecca Goldthorpe
R.E. Pernicano
Rebecca Sarabia
Rebecca Wojturska
Rian Desourdie
Dr. Ronna Privett
Rosie Hughes
Ross Sayers
Rowan Hollinshead
Ruby Kelly
Ryan Power
S. Chen

Sabrina Young

Sally Logue Post

Sam Canning

Samantha Lack

Sandra Corbett

Sanskar Wagley

Sara

Sara Hunt

Sarah Danielle

Sarah Garnham

Sarah E. M. Mason

Sarah Fae and Kathryn Holeman

Sarah Martin

Sasha Paduganan Lucero

Scott Brayford

Sharlan

Shenai Alonge

S. L. Morrison

Sonya Young

Sophie Wilson

Stacey Welchley

Stephanie Cargill-Greer

Stephanie Grisby

Tara Fitzpatrick

Taralyn Brinks

Taylor McAlpine

Taylor Mulholland

Ted Lankester
The Creative Fund by BackerKit
Thuy-Duong Ha
Toby Millard
Trisha Martin
Tristan Gray
Vanessa Jenkins Burnley
Vanessa Ta
Vicki Hsu
Wendy Reynolds
Yasmin Hackett
Yvonne Murray
Zavier B.
Zia Striowsky
Zoë King
Zoe Louise Tongue

ACKNOWLEDGEMENTS

I want to take a moment to thank the people who helped in the creation of *We Are Not Shadows*. First, thank you to my dear friend Alice Piotrowska, who helped in the selection process and endured my many frantic texts about the book. You are truly a gem. Second, thank you to the creative hands this book went through, from start to finish. Thank you to Curtis Spivey for the outstanding promotional Kickstarter video for the book, to Kristen Susienka for her wonderful editorial work, and to Will Dady of Renard Press for his beautiful typesetting. Finally, thank you to the many family, friends, and colleagues who encouraged me to launch Folkways Press and this anthology. I look forward to the future of the press and the many books to come.